THE OFFICIAL

JOHN WAYNE
REAL AMERICAN
GRILLING

MANLY MEALS AND BACKYARD FAVORITES FROM DUKE'S FAMILY TO YOURS

John Wayne, Gail Russell and Irene Rich in a scene from *Angel and the Badman* (1947), directed by James Edward Grant.

John Wayne during the filming of *The Undefeated* (1969).

TABLE OF CONTENTS

pg. 186

pg. 60

John Wayne and his children Melinda, Patrick, Toni and Michael at the annual Sheriff's Rodeo at the Los Angeles Coliseum, August 14, 1949.

MY FATHER LOVED BRINGING PEOPLE TOGETHER.

WHETHER HE WAS FILMING the latest ode to the Old West, directing a blockbuster homage to our country's heroes at the Alamo or entertaining loved ones aboard the *Wild Goose*, above all, Duke understood the value of community. As a proud American, he treasured every opportunity to create a feeling of togetherness by cooking in the great outdoors in observance of this nation's beloved pastime. I'm pleased to share with you this collection of delicious flame-grilled recipes, techniques and a Wayne family tip or two on how to make the most of your meal. There's even an assortment of little known Duke facts and grilling trivia sure to keep you on your toes while you keep an eye on your steaks. We hope this book will inspire your family to create new traditions to be proud of, just like Duke would want.

DIG IN.

GRABBING A MOUTHFUL

Duke enjoying a John Wayne-sized serving of sausage. Sausage is great for anyone grilling in a hurry, especially if you split them open lengthwise, which reduces cook time to five minutes.

GRILLING BASICS

COOKING OVER AN OPEN FLAME COMES WITH GREAT RESPONSIBILITY, AND IT'S NOT FOR THE FAINT OF HEART. TAKE A NOTE FROM DUKE'S BOOK AND USE THESE TRICKS TO MASTER YOUR GRILLING GAME.

Lighting Your Grill

To get started, remove all ash and grease from your grill. A brush with metal bristles will scrape up all the charred fat and remove last month's flavors from your grill. If you don't have a grill brush handy, though, don't sweat it. Crumple some aluminum foil into a ball and handle it between your tongs. If you're using a gas grill, you're ready to turn it on. If not, add some charcoal to your grill and prep it to burn. The amount you'll use will vary depending on the size of your grill, but as a rule of thumb, try to make two full, even layers of briquettes. Once you've got your layers, stack them into a cone shape in the middle of your grill. In stormy or windy weather, you'll want to use a few more briquettes so your grill stays nice and hot. Next, pour lighter fluid on the coals, paying special attention to the middle of the cone. Use about a quarter-cup of lighter fluid (60ml) per pound (450g) of charcoal. Wait about 30 seconds for the lighter fluid to soak into the charcoal, then light with a long match or compact roll of newspaper.

Keeping Your Grill Perfect

An optimal grill means your setup is hot, clean and well-lubricated, all of which help minimize outside flavors imparted by the grill and maximize the quality of your meal. Along with preheating and cleaning your grill as just described, to keep your grill slick and cut down on sticky, charred food bits that stick around after you've dished out your meal, look no further than a paper towel covered in oil. Just place the paper towel in your tongs and rub down the grill with cooking oil before you fire it up.

Direct or Indirect Heat

Before you start cooking, you'll have to make a decision between direct and indirect heat. Foods that take less than 30 minutes to cook over flame are best cooked directly. These include boneless chicken, steaks, fish fillets, hamburgers and hot dogs. All you really have to do is toss them on the grill and try not to torch them. Foods that take longer than 30 minutes are best grilled with indirect heat. Whole turkeys, bone-in chicken, brisket and other larger fare should be placed above a drip pan to create an effect similar to oven-roasting. If you're using charcoal, arrange your briquettes on the lower level against the drip pan before placing your meat on the grill. You can add water to the drip pan to provide some extra moisture or get a little creative if you like and add something like apple juice for a bit of flavor.

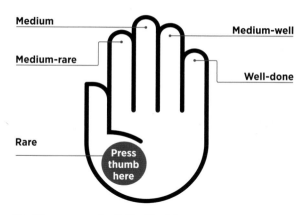

Medium

Medium-well

Medium-rare

Well-done

Rare

Press thumb here

No Thermometer? No Problem.

No one's going to bat an eye if you grab a state-of-the-art probe thermometer to ensure you've got the temperature just right. But you can also use the thermometer God gave you: your hands. If you're cooking 1-inch slices of steak, rare meat will take about 15 to 20 minutes over a grill that is 350 degrees Fahrenheit; if you can only stand to hold your hand over the coals for around seven seconds, it's cooking at 350 degrees. At this temperature, a steak cooked to medium will be done in less than 25 minutes while a well-done one will take up to 30. To check the temperature of the meat, hold your left hand down flat, palm side up, and press the thumb of your other hand into the fleshiest part of the palm (see chart above). The softness of that spot will mimic the feel of a rare steak. Next, touch your left thumb to the pads of each of your other fingers on your left hand while keeping your right thumb on your palm. By moving from the index finger to the pinky, the pad on your left hand will feel similar to a medium-rare, medium, medium-well and well-done steak. And remember: You can always toss a steak back on the grill to bring it to a higher temperature—but you can't un-cook charbroiled meat.

Putting Out the Fire

First, cover your grill and close the vents if you've got 'em. For gas, turn off all your burners, then make sure to close off your LP tank as well if applicable. If using charcoal, allow your coals to burn out, then let the ashes cool for at least 48 hours and dispose of them in a container that isn't flammable. If you find you must cut that 48 hours short, remove each brick one at a time with long tongs and submerge them in either water or sand.

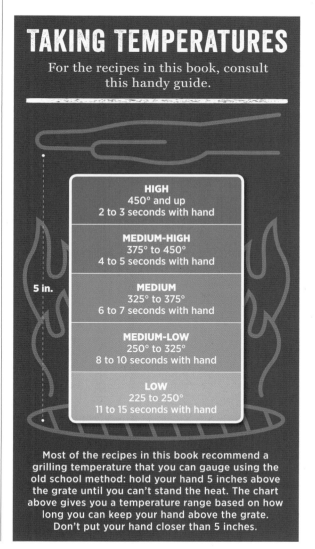

TAKING TEMPERATURES

For the recipes in this book, consult this handy guide.

5 in.

HIGH
450° and up
2 to 3 seconds with hand

MEDIUM-HIGH
375° to 450°
4 to 5 seconds with hand

MEDIUM
325° to 375°
6 to 7 seconds with hand

MEDIUM-LOW
250° to 325°
8 to 10 seconds with hand

LOW
225 to 250°
11 to 15 seconds with hand

Most of the recipes in this book recommend a grilling temperature that you can gauge using the old school method: hold your hand 5 inches above the grate until you can't stand the heat. The chart above gives you a temperature range based on how long you can keep your hand above the grate. Don't put your hand closer than 5 inches.

John Wayne during the filming of *The Undefeated* (1969). The film's stampede scene featured 3,000 horses, and when filming wrapped, the crew discovered 60 had gone missing.

Sweet Chili-Glazed
Drumettes, p. 32

STARTERS

Get your guests all fired up for the cookout with these easy apps
that are sure to impress any crowd.

Epic Jalapeño Poppers

Zesty Buffalo Wings

Grilled Flatbreads

Grilled Tomato Crostini

Grilled Clams with Lemon Butter Sauce

Salsa Verde

***King of the Pecos* Buffalo Peppers**

Sweet Chili-Glazed Drumettes

Campfire Queso

Quick Draw Nachos

EPIC JALAPEÑO POPPERS

Watch out—when it comes to fiery flavor, these peppers pack a punch!

PROVISIONS

12	large jalapeño peppers
4	oz. cream cheese, softened
½	cup cheddar cheese, grated
8	slices thin-cut bacon

PREP

1. Prepare grill for direct heat and preheat to medium.

2. Cut peppers in half lengthwise, then scrape out the seeds and veins.

3. Combine the cream and cheddar cheese in a mixing bowl. Divide the mixture evenly among the pepper halves.

4. Cut each bacon slice into thirds and wrap the peppers, making sure the bacon "seam" is on the bottom of the pepper, then place them in a cast iron skillet. Place on the grill, cover the lid and cook for 15 to 20 minutes or until the bacon is browned and the cheese melted.

MAKES 24 POPPERS

John Wayne and Capucine in *North to Alaska* (1960).

DID YOU KNOW?

John Wayne's co-star in *North to Alaska* (1960), Capucine, later appeared as Simone Clouseau in *The Pink Panther* (1963).

ZESTY BUFFALO WINGS

If you love all things spicy just like Duke, then you know no cookout is complete without a hearty helping of these backyard favorites.

PROVISIONS

BLUE CHEESE DIP

½	cup sour cream
¼	cup mayonnaise
4	oz. crumbled blue cheese
1	Tbsp. milk
	Salt and pepper, to taste

WINGS

2	tsp. kosher or fine sea salt
1	tsp. black pepper
1	tsp. garlic powder
3	lb. whole chicken wings
	Vegetable oil
6	Tbsp. unsalted butter
⅓	cup hot sauce
	Celery sticks
	Carrot sticks

John Wayne in
The Big Trail
(1930).

PREP

1. Stir all the dip ingredients together and refrigerate until serving time.

2. Prepare grill for direct and indirect heat and preheat to medium.

3. In a small bowl, combine the salt, pepper and garlic powder. Pat the wings dry with paper towels and sprinkle all over with seasoning. Brush the wings with vegetable oil.

4. Place the wings skin side down over the direct heat, crowding them together in a single layer so that they touch, then cook with the lid up for 5 minutes. Flip the wings over and move to the indirect side of the grill, lower the lid and cook for 20 minutes.

5. In a small pan over low heat, heat the butter and hot sauce together, stir to combine and pour into a large bowl. Add the wings to the bowl with the hot sauce mixture and toss to coat. Place the wings back on the direct heat side of the grill and grill for another 2 minutes per side or until crispy and charred. Toss the wings in the hot sauce mixture one more time and serve with the blue cheese dip, celery sticks and carrot sticks.

SERVES 8

★ AMERICAN GRILL FACTS

Originating in Buffalo, New York, Buffalo wings are believed to have been created in 1964 at a restaurant called Anchor Bar.

John Wayne visits
Monument Valley
in 1971.

GRILLED FLATBREADS

There's no need to fire up the oven when it comes to whipping up these no-frills flatbreads.

PROVISIONS

- ¾ cup all-purpose flour, plus more for dusting
- 1 tsp. baking powder
- ½ tsp. kosher or fine sea salt
- 5 Tbsp. yogurt
- 1 Tbsp. honey
- 1 Tbsp. olive oil
- ¼ cup prepared pesto
- 4 thin slices fresh mozzarella cheese
- 1 roma tomato, sliced

PREP

1. Prepare grill for direct heat and preheat to high.

2. In a medium mixing bowl, whisk together the flour, baking powder and salt. Add the yogurt, honey and olive oil, then mix until it forms into a dough. Divide the dough into two equal portions. Lightly flour a work surface and roll the dough into an 8- by 5-inch oval slightly less than ¼-inch thick.

3. Grill for 2 to 3 minutes or until golden brown. Flip and cook for another 2 minutes. Spread pesto on each flatbread, top with cheese and tomato slices, close the lid and cook for another minute or until the cheese starts to melt. Serve.

SERVES 2

GRILLED TOMATO CROSTINI

Serve up the taste of summer with this rustic, easy-to-make appetizer that'll have you dreaming of sun-drenched Tuscan villas.

PROVISIONS

- 1 pint cherry or grape tomatoes, cut in half
- 2 cloves garlic, minced

  Olive oil

  Kosher or fine sea salt

  Black pepper

- 1 baguette, cut into ½-inch slices on the diagonal

  Basil leaves, for garnish

PREP

1. Prepare grill for direct heat and preheat to medium.

2. Take a sheet of heavy-duty aluminum foil, fold up the four sides to create a basket, then place the grape tomatoes in the center. Add the garlic, 1 Tbsp. olive oil, 1 tsp. salt and ½ tsp. pepper. Fold the sides of the foil together, sealing the package.

3. Place the package on the grill for 10 to 15 minutes or until the tomatoes are softened and juicy. Remove from the grill and let cool slightly.

4. Meanwhile, brush the baguette slices with olive oil on both sides and season lightly with salt and pepper. Grill over direct heat until toasted, top with tomatoes, garnish with basil and serve.

SERVES 4

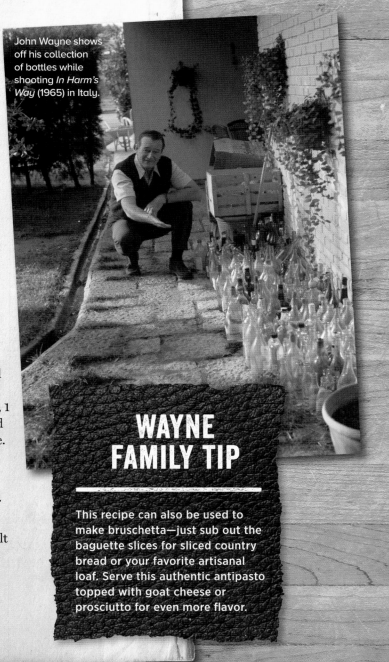

John Wayne shows off his collection of bottles while shooting *In Harm's Way* (1965) in Italy.

WAYNE FAMILY TIP

This recipe can also be used to make bruschetta—just sub out the baguette slices for sliced country bread or your favorite artisanal loaf. Serve this authentic antipasto topped with goat cheese or prosciutto for even more flavor.

GRILLED CLAMS
WITH LEMON BUTTER SAUCE

Good food doesn't need a whole lot of fixins to shine, so skip the linguine and throw these clams straight on the grill.

PROVISIONS

4	Tbsp. melted butter
1	Tbsp. chopped flat leaf parsley
1	Tbsp. fresh lemon juice
¼	tsp. salt
⅛	tsp. pepper
24	littleneck clams, scrubbed
	Lemon wedges, for serving

PREP

1. Combine the melted butter, parsley, lemon juice, salt and pepper and keep warm.

2. Prepare grill for direct heat and preheat to high. Place the clams in a single layer directly on the grill rack. Grill just until the clams open—this will take between 5 to 10 minutes.

3. Using tongs, carefully remove the clam shells from the grill and place on a serving platter, trying not to lose the liquid inside the shells. Discard any clams that do not open. Spoon some of the lemon butter into each clam and serve.

SERVES 6

John Wayne and Nan Grey in *The Sea Spoilers* (1936).

★
AMERICAN GRILL FACTS

Other good quahogs for grilling are countnecks and cherrystones, which are slightly larger than littenecks.

PRIVATE
DOCK
KEEP OFF

John Wayne visits his yacht, the *Wild Goose*, in June 1967. Duke purchased the decommissioned U.S. Navy minesweeper five years prior.

SALSA VERDE

Start your fiesta off with a bang courtesy of the jalapeño in this colorful, citrusy salsa that pairs well with just about anything.

PROVISIONS

1½	lb. tomatillos
1	medium white onion, thickly sliced
2	poblano peppers, cut in half, seeds and veins removed (leave seeds in for spicier sauce)
2	jalapeño peppers, cut in half, seeds and veins removed (leave seeds in for spicier sauce)
2	Tbsp. vegetable oil
2	tsp. garlic powder
1	tsp. kosher or fine sea salt
½	tsp. black pepper
	Juice of 1 lime (2 Tbsp.)
½	cup fresh cilantro leaves
	Tortilla chips

PREP

1. Prepare grill for direct heat and preheat to medium.

2. Remove the husks from the tomatillos, rinse and cut in half. Place in a large bowl along with the onion, peppers, oil, garlic powder, salt and pepper then toss to coat. Grill, turning occasionally, until the vegetables are soft and charred, about 10 minutes.

3. Transfer the vegetables into a food processor or blender. Add the lime juice and cilantro and pulse several times until you have a thick, slightly chunky sauce. Can be used immediately or stored in a covered glass container for up to one week. The salsa is good hot or cold. Serve with tortilla chips.

MAKES ABOUT 2 CUPS

John Wayne in *Somewhere in Sonora* (1933).

KING OF THE PECOS BUFFALO PEPPERS

You'll be riding tall in the saddle after you dish out these mouthwatering grilled peppers to a hungry crew.

PROVISIONS

12-14	mini sweet peppers*
4	oz. cream cheese, room temperature
1	cup cooked, shredded chicken
½	cup shredded sharp cheddar cheese
¼	cup Buffalo sauce, plus more for serving
	Ranch dressing
	Fresh cilantro leaves, chopped

PREP

1. Cut ⅓ off of each pepper lengthwise, then finely chop the flesh you cut off of the peppers. Use a small spoon to remove any seeds and excess ribs from the peppers. Set aside.

2. Place the chopped peppers in a mixing bowl with the cream cheese, chicken, cheddar cheese and Buffalo sauce. Mix well. Stuff the filling into the peppers making sure to fill all the nooks and crannies. Refrigerate for 1 hour (or longer if needed).

3. Prepare grill for direct heat and preheat to medium, about 450 degrees F. Oil the grates. Place the peppers on the grill, cradling them between two grates to hold them upright. Cover and grill for 5 to 7 minutes or until the cheese is melted and the peppers are soft and charred. If you want the top of the cheese browned, place under a hot broiler for 1 to 2 minutes.

4. Drizzle some ranch dressing and Buffalo sauce over the peppers and garnish with cilantro.

MAKES 12–14

*NOTE The rounder type of pepper works best as opposed to the flatter variety, but if you can only find the latter, you'll need twice as many peppers for this recipe.

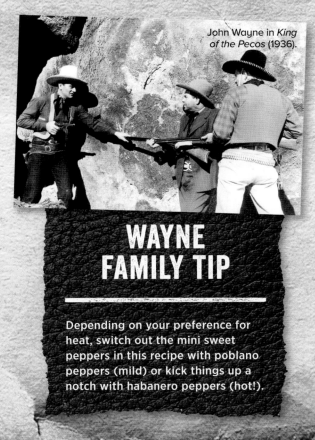

John Wayne in *King of the Pecos* (1936).

WAYNE FAMILY TIP

Depending on your preference for heat, switch out the mini sweet peppers in this recipe with poblano peppers (mild) or kick things up a notch with habanero peppers (hot!).

SWEET CHILI-GLAZED DRUMETTES

Grillmasters and crafty chefs take note: the sweet chili sauce-based marinade on these drummettes also goes well with grilled fish or pork chops.

PROVISIONS

½   **cup ketchup**

¼   **cup sweet chili sauce**

2   **Tbsp. low sodium soy sauce**

¾   **tsp. ground ginger**

½   **tsp. garlic powder**

3   **lb. chicken wing drumettes**

1   **green onion, very finely minced**

    Ranch dressing, for serving

PREP

1. Combine the ketchup, chili sauce, soy sauce, ginger and garlic powder and mix well. Pour ¾ of the mixture into a large food storage bag, reserving the rest. Add the chicken wings, seal the bag and toss several times to coat. Let the chicken wings marinate for 20 minutes at room temperature or for 4 to 8 hours in the refrigerator.

2. Prepare grill for direct heat and preheat to medium. Oil the grates.

3. Using barbecue tongs, remove the drumettes from the bag and place on the grill. Discard the marinade in the bag. Cover and grill for 10 minutes. Brush the drumettes with the reserved marinade, then flip

John Wayne and Dona Drake in *Without Reservations* (1946).

them over and brush with more of the reserved marinade. Cover and grill for another 10 minutes. Give the wings a final brush of the marinade, flip and cook for another 1 to 2 minutes or until done and nicely charred. Place on a serving platter, sprinkle with the green onion and serve with ranch dressing on the side.

SERVES 6

CAMPFIRE QUESO

This bubbling hot cheesy favorite is sure to satisfy even the pickiest cowpokes.

PROVISIONS

1	lb. chorizo, removed from casings and crumbled
16	oz. Velveeta cheese, diced into cubes
1	(10-oz.) can diced tomatoes and chilies, undrained
2	cups shredded Mexican cheese blend
2	jalapeño peppers, sliced
½	cup fresh cilantro leaves, roughly chopped

PREP

1. Prepare grill for direct and indirect heat and preheat to medium-low (300 degrees F).

2. Spray a cast iron skillet with cooking spray. Cook the sausage over the direct side of the grill. Discard any fat. Place the rest of the ingredients in the pan, cover with foil and place over indirect heat. Cook for 30 minutes, stirring every 10 minutes.

3. Serve with tortilla chips, crusty bread or fresh vegetables.

SERVES 12

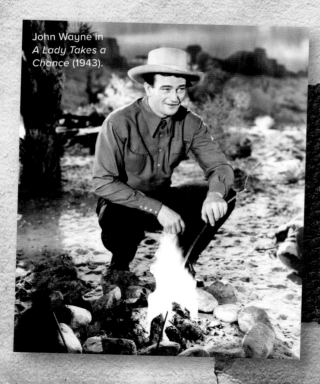

John Wayne in *A Lady Takes a Chance* (1943).

WAYNE FAMILY TIP

If you're looking for easy cleanup, you're in luck: this tasty starter can also be made in a 9- by 12-inch disposable foil pan. Just be sure to cook the chorizo before adding it to the pan.

QUICK DRAW NACHOS

If you want a campground take on a south of the border standby, this appetizer comes together faster than you can say "Got any seconds?"

PROVISIONS

QUICK PICKLED RED ONIONS

1	small red onion
½	cup grenadine
½	cup red wine vinegar

NACHOS

8	oz. corn tortilla chips
2	cups shredded cooked chicken
½	cup barbecue sauce
2	cups grated cheddar or Mexican blend cheese
	Quick pickled red onions (see below), drained
¼	cup pickled jalapeño slices, drained

John Wayne in
Ride Him, Cowboy
(1932).

PREP

1. To make the pickled red onions, cut the onion in half and thinly slice. Combine the grenadine and vinegar in a small pot. Bring to a boil over high heat. Take off the heat, add the onions and let sit for 10 to 15 minutes. Can be used immediately or stored, covered in the refrigerator for 2 weeks.

2. Prepare grill for indirect heat. Place the tortilla chips in a large cast iron skillet or disposable foil pan.

3. Combine the chicken and barbecue sauce and scatter the mixture over the chips. Top with cheese. Grill with the lid closed for 5 to 10 minutes or until the cheese has melted.

4. Top with the pickled red onions and jalapeño slices before serving.

SERVES 8

Bistecca Alla
Fiorentina,
p. 76

BEEF

If you're searching for the quintessential grilled meat, feast your eyes on John Wayne's favorite by a long shot.

The Best Darn Cowboy Steak

Fiesta Fajitas

Dawn Rider Rib-Eye with BBQ Sauce

Rancher Rib-Eye with Onion Jam and Blue Cheese

Sweet and Spicy Filet Mignon

Gaucho Filet with Balsamic Glaze and Goat Cheese

Skirt Steak with Chimichurri Sauce

Flying Leathernecks Bacon-Wrapped Filet

Star Packer Street Tacos

Rodeo Rider Beef Ribs

Pilar's Carne Asada

Lucky Texan London Broil

The Conqueror's Steak Kebabs with Tarragon Aioli

Grilled Sirloin with Poblano Pepper Sauce

Yakima Canutt's Pepper Crusted T-Bone Steak

Cheese-and-Red-Pepper-Stuffed Flank Steak

Bistecca alla Fiorentina

THE BEST DARN COWBOY STEAK

After a hard day's work, nothing fills you up quite like a classic bone-in cowboy steak, plain and simple. Accept no substitutes.

PROVISIONS

- 1 (2 ½–3 lb.) cowboy steak
- Kosher or fine sea salt
- Black pepper
- Vegetable oil
- 2 oz. butter
- 2 cloves garlic, smashed

PREP

1. Remove steak from refrigerator and let sit at room temperature for 1 hour. Season generously on both sides with salt and pepper.

2. Prepare grill for direct and indirect heat and preheat to low (225 degrees F). Oil the grates.

3. Place steak on the indirect heat side of the grill, close the lid and cook until the steak reaches an internal temperature of 125 degrees F for medium-rare, 30 to 40 minutes.

4. Melt butter with the smashed garlic cloves.

5. When the steak comes to temperature, place it over direct heat for 3 to 4 minutes, flipping every 20 seconds.

6. Remove the steak from the grill, brush with the butter and garlic mixture and let rest 10 to 15 minutes before serving.

SERVES 2

John Wayne in *The Cowboys* (1972).

WAYNE FAMILY TIP

This method of reverse searing your steak—cooking it over a low temperature for a long period of time before searing it on high heat for a few minutes—ensures your steaks stay tender. It works well for other thick-cut steaks like the T-bone, porterhouse, filet mignon and more.

FIESTA FAJITAS

Start your party on a high note with a sizzling plate of this flame-grilled skirt steak. Load up a warm tortilla and go to town.

PROVISIONS

MARINADE

- ¾ **cup olive oil**
- ½ **cup orange juice (from 1 large orange)**
- ¼ **cup lime juice (from 2–3 limes)**
- 1 **jalapeño, minced**
- 2 **cloves garlic, minced**
- 1 **tsp. ground cumin**
- 1 **tsp. dried oregano**
- 1 **tsp. kosher or fine sea salt**
- ½ **tsp. pepper**

FAJITAS

- 2 **lb. skirt steak**
- 1 **large onion, thinly sliced**
- 1 **green bell pepper, seeded, deveined and thinly sliced**
- 1 **red bell pepper, seeded, deveined and thinly sliced**
- 1 **yellow or orange bell pepper, seeded deveined and thinly sliced**
- **Vegetable oil**
- **Salt and pepper, to taste**
- 12 **flour tortillas or 24 corn tortillas, warmed**

FOR SERVING, OPTIONAL

- **Salsa**
- **Sour cream**
- **Avocado slices**
- **Guacamole**
- **Grated cheese**

John Wayne and Syd Saylor in *Born to the West* (1937).

PREP

1. Combine all the marinade ingredients in a mixing bowl and whisk well.

2. Place the steak in a large food storage bag, pour in half the marinade and seal.

3. Place the onions and peppers in another large food storage bag, pour in the rest of the marinade and seal. Place the steak and vegetables in the refrigerator, laying the bags flat, and marinate for 4 hours, flipping the bags occasionally.

4. Prepare the grill for direct heat and preheat to medium-high.

5. Drain and discard the marinade from the steak and vegetables. Brush the grates with oil and cook the steak 2 to 3 minutes per side with the lid closed. Remove from grill, place on a cutting board, cover with foil and let rest for 10 minutes.

6. While the steak is resting, prepare the vegetables by placing a cast iron skillet directly on the grill and letting it heat. Add 1 Tbsp. of vegetable oil and let that get hot. Add the vegetables and cook, stirring occasionally, until softened, about 7 minutes. Alternatively, you can cook the vegetables on the stove.

7. Slice the steak thinly, season to taste with salt and pepper and serve with the vegetables and warmed tortillas.

SERVES 6

DAWN RIDER RIB-EYE
WITH BBQ SAUCE

If you're hankering for big, bold flavor, this savory steak can't be beat.

PROVISIONS

- 1   dried ancho chile pepper
- 1½   Tbsp. smoked paprika
- 1   Tbsp. plus 1 tsp. kosher salt, divided
- 1   Tbsp. onion powder
- 1   Tbsp. garlic powder
- 1   Tbsp. plus ½ tsp. black pepper, divided
- 1   Tbsp. plus 1 tsp. dried oregano, divided
- 3   Tbsp. brown sugar, divided
- 2   tsp. dried cumin, divided
- 4   rib-eye steaks, about 1 inch thick
-     Olive oil
-     Vegetable oil
- 3   plum tomatoes
- ½   red onion, cut into ½ inch slices
- 2   garlic cloves, smashed
- 3   Tbsp. apple cider vinegar

PREP

1. Cover the ancho chile with ¾ cup boiling water and let sit for 30 minutes to soften.

2. In a small bowl, combine the paprika with 1 Tbsp. salt, onion and garlic powders, 1 Tbsp. pepper, 1 Tbsp. oregano, 1 Tbsp. brown sugar and 1 tsp. cumin. Pat the steaks dry, brush with olive oil and season generously with the dry rub on all sides. Let the steaks sit at room temperature for 30 to 40 minutes.

John Wayne in *The Dawn Rider* (1935).

3. Prepare the grill for direct heat. Oil the grates.

4. Cut the tomatoes in half lengthwise. Brush the cut sides and the onion slices with olive oil. Place on the grill over direct heat and grill with the lid closed for 4 to 5 minutes per side or until charred and softened. Remove the ancho chile from the water, remove the stem and seeds and place in a blender with the water it was soaking in, the tomatoes, onions, 1 tsp. salt, 1 tsp. pepper, 2 Tbsp. brown sugar, 1 tsp. cumin, garlic cloves and apple cider vinegar. Blend until smooth. Pour half the sauce into a serving bowl to serve with the steaks.

5. Grill steaks over direct heat for 4 minutes, flip and grill for 4 to 5 minutes or until they reach 130 degrees F for medium-rare, basting with the sauce frequently. Let steaks rest for 10 minutes. Serve with the sauce.

SERVES 4

RANCHER RIB-EYE
WITH ONION JAM AND BLUE CHEESE

Blue cheese isn't for everyone, and that's OK; the sweet onion jam in this recipe balances out the sharpness of the cheese for a combo that'll make your head spin.

PROVISIONS

- **4** **(1¼–1½ inch thick) boneless rib-eye steaks**
- **2** **Tbsp. olive oil, plus more for the steak**

    Black pepper
- **3** **sweet onions, peeled, halved and sliced ¼ inch thick**
- **1** **tsp. kosher or fine sea salt, plus more for the steak**
- **2** **cloves garlic, minced**
- **1** **jalapeño, seeded, deveined and finely chopped**
- **¼** **cup balsamic vinegar**
- **2** **Tbsp. brown sugar**
- **¼** **tsp. chopped fresh parsley**
- **4** **oz. blue cheese crumbles**

John Wayne, son Patrick and Jacquetta LeForce, the daughter of the ranch manager of 26 Bar Ranch.

PREP

1. Remove steaks from refrigerator at least 20 minutes before grilling. Brush both sides with olive oil and season generously with salt and pepper.

2. Prepare grill for direct heat and preheat to high. Oil the grates.

3. Place a large cast iron skillet on the grill, add 2 Tbsp. olive oil and heat. Add the onions, 1 tsp. salt, ½ tsp. pepper, garlic, jalapeño, vinegar and brown sugar. Cook with the lid closed, stirring occasionally until it reaches a jam-like consistency, about 20 minutes. Stir in the parsley, remove from the grill and let cool.

4. Place the steaks on the grill and cook for 5 minutes. Flip and grill for another 3 to 4 minutes or until they reach an internal temperature of 130 degrees F for medium-rare. Remove from grill and let rest for 5 to 10 minutes.

5. Top the steaks with the onion jam and blue cheese crumbles.

SERVES 4

John Wayne and
Sheila Terry in
Haunted Gold (1932).

SWEET AND SPICY FILET MIGNON

Honey, aka liquid gold, isn't just key to this irresistible marinade—it makes for a melt-in-your-mouth steak, too!

PROVISIONS

- ¼ **cup Dijon mustard**
- ¼ **cup honey**
- 4 **(1¼–1½ inch thick) filet mignon steaks**
- **Olive oil**
- **Kosher or fine sea salt**
- **Black pepper**
- **Vegetable oil**

PREP

1. Combine the mustard and honey. Set aside.

2. Remove steaks from refrigerator 20 minutes before grilling. Brush both sides with oil. Season generously with salt and pepper.

3. Prepare grill for direct heat and preheat to medium-high. Oil the grates.

4. Grill the steaks for 5 minutes with the lid closed. Brush with the honey mustard sauce, flip and grill for another 3 to 4 minutes or until an internal temperature of 130 degrees F is achieved. Brush with more sauce before serving.

SERVES 4

DID YOU KNOW?

Sheila Terry also appeared as John Wayne's leading lady in two other Westerns: *The Lawless Frontier* (1934) and *'Neath the Arizona Skies* (1934).

GAUCHO FILET
WITH BALSAMIC GLAZE AND GOAT CHEESE

You don't need access to a Michelin-star chef's kitchen (or pantry) to throw down delectable meals for the whole family. Mealtime doesn't need to be complicated. This dish comes together with just five ingredients.

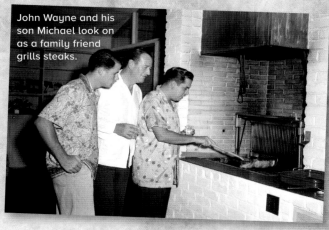

John Wayne and his son Michael look on as a family friend grills steaks.

PROVISIONS

4 (1¼–1½ inch thick) filet mignon steaks

Montreal steak seasoning (see right)

Olive oil

Vegetable oil

2 oz. soft goat cheese, crumbled

2 Tbsp. balsamic glaze (see right)

PREP

1. Remove steaks from refrigerator and let sit at room temperature for 20 minutes. Brush both sides with olive oil and season with Montreal steak seasoning.

2. Prepare grill for direct heat and preheat to medium-high. Brush the grates with vegetable oil.

3. Grill the steaks with the lid closed for 5 minutes. Flip, cook with lid closed for 2 minutes, top with cheese and cook for another 1 to 2 minutes or until the steaks reach an internal temperature of 130 degrees F for medium rare and the cheese is just starting to melt. Let rest for 5 minutes.

4. Drizzle with balsamic glaze and serve.

SERVES 4

MONTREAL STEAK SEASONING

2 Tbsp. coarse ground black pepper

2 Tbsp. paprika

2 Tbsp. kosher salt

2 Tbsp. garlic powder

1 Tbsp. onion powder

1 Tbsp. ground coriander

1 Tbsp. dried dill

1 Tbsp. crushed red pepper flakes

Combine all ingredients in a small bowl. Store in an airtight container for up to 6 months. Makes ¾ cup.

BALSAMIC GLAZE

Place ½ cup balsamic vinegar in a small saucepan and bring to a boil over high heat. Reduce heat to a simmer and cook uncovered, stirring occasionally, until the mixture is syrupy and reduced to about 2 Tbsp., 12 to 15 minutes. Makes 2 Tbsp.

John Wayne greets his fans outside Grauman's Chinese Theatre in Hollywood, California, on January 25, 1950. Instead of the usual handprints, the icon left his footprints as well as a fist print.

SKIRT STEAK
WITH CHIMICHURRI SAUCE

Send your taste buds on a trip to South America with this bright, citrusy meal that incorporates the quintessential Argentinian condiment. Buen provecho!

PROVISIONS

2	cups (packed) flat leaf parsley
2	cloves garlic, chopped
1	tsp. dried oregano
1	tsp. kosher or fine sea salt, plus more to taste
½	tsp. pepper, plus more to taste
½	tsp. crushed red pepper flakes
4	Tbsp. lemon juice (2 lemons)
2	Tbsp. white wine or sherry vinegar
⅔	cup olive oil

STEAK

2	lb. skirt steak
	Vegetable oil

Duke and Pilar at a dinner party c. 1955.

PREP

1. Combine the parsley, garlic, oregano, 1 tsp. salt, ½ tsp. pepper, red pepper flakes, lemon juice and vinegar in a blender or food processor and process until almost smooth. Add the olive oil and blend. Taste and add more salt and pepper if desired. Take ½ cup of the chimichurri to marinate the steak and reserve the rest for serving.

2. Coat the steak with ½ cup chimichurri, rubbing it into the meat. Cover with plastic wrap and let sit at room temperature for 20 to 30 minutes.

3. Prepare grill for direct heat and preheat to medium-high. Brush the grates with oil.

4. Place the steak on the grill and grill 2 to 3 minutes per side with the lid closed. Let sit for 5 to 10 minutes before slicing.

5. Slice the steak and serve with the reserved chimichurri sauce.

SERVES 4

FLYING LEATHERNECKS BACON-WRAPPED FILET

No need to go over the top with frilly fixings—this steak's outer layer of crispy bacon will have your taste buds soaring to new heights.

PROVISIONS

- 4 (1¼–1½ inch thick) filet mignon steaks
- Olive oil
- Kosher or fine sea salt
- Black pepper
- 4 slices thick-cut bacon
- Vegetable oil
- Chive compound butter (see right)

PREP

1. Remove steaks from the refrigerator and let sit at room temperature for 20 minutes. Lightly brush both sides with olive oil and season lightly with salt and pepper. Wrap a slice of bacon around each steak and secure with butcher's twine.

2. Prepare grill for direct heat and preheat to medium-high heat. Oil the grates with vegetable oil.

3. Grill for 4 to 5 minutes per side or until the steaks reach an internal temperature of 130 degrees F for medium-rare. If the bacon is not crisp enough, use a pair of long tongs to hold the steaks over the grill with the bacon facing the heat to crisp it up. Let steaks rest for 5 to 10 minutes before serving. Cut compound butter into four slices and place one on each steak.

SERVES 4

John Wayne in
Flying Leathernecks
(1951).

CHIVE COMPOUND BUTTER

Mix 4 Tbsp. salted butter, softened and 1 tsp. minced chives in a bowl. Place on wax paper, roll into a log and twist the ends to seal. Refrigerate until solid, about 1 hour.

STAR PACKER STREET TACOS

Add some authentic south-of-the-border flair to your party spread with these spicy bites you can savor from the comforts of home...or wherever you roam.

PROVISIONS

SALSA

- 2 jalapeños
- 6 plum tomatoes, cut in half lengthwise
- 1 small red onion, sliced ¼-inch thick
- 4 Tbsp. lime juice (2 limes)
- ½ tsp. kosher or fine sea salt
- ½ cup cilantro leaves
- Vegetable oil

TACOS

- 12 corn tortillas
- Vegetable oil
- 1½ lb. flank or skirt steak
- Kosher or fine sea salt
- Pepper
- ½ small red or white onion, finely diced
- ½ cup cilantro leaves, finely chopped

Yakima Canutt and John Wayne in *The Star Packer* (1934).

PREP

1. Prepare grill for direct heat and preheat to high.

2. Place the jalapeños directly on the grill. Cook with lid down, turning occasionally, until the skin is charred all over, about 10 to 12 minutes. Take off the grill, place in a small bowl and cover with plastic wrap. Let sit for at least 5 minutes.

3. Brush the cut sides of the tomatoes with oil and place directly on the grill. Brush both sides of the onion with oil and place directly on the grill. Grill with the lid closed until the tomatoes are a little charred and starting to soften, about 10 minutes. Grill the onions, flipping once, until charred and beginning to soften. Keep the grill lit.

4. Rub the jalapeños to remove the charred skin. For a mild salsa, cut in half and scrape out the seeds. Place in a blender or food processor with the grilled tomatoes and onions. Add the lime juice and salt and blend until smooth, scraping down the sides of the container as needed. Add the cilantro and pulse several times. Place in a serving bowl.

5. Wrap the tortillas in foil and place on the top rack of the grill or on the coolest side to warm them.

6. Brush the grill grates with oil.

7. Season the steak with salt and pepper and grill with the lid open for 2 minutes per side. Let sit for 5 minutes before serving. Cut the steak into thin slices.

8. Serve the meat in the tortillas with the onion and cilantro and the salsa on the side.

SERVES 4 (3 TACOS PER PERSON)

Jean Arthur and John Wayne in *A Lady Takes a Chance* (1943).

RODEO RIDER BEEF RIBS

Whether you consider yourself a greenhorn or a grill master extraordinaire, when your guests catch a whiff of this meal, they'll be barrel racing through the backyard to be first in line.

PROVISIONS

- 5 lb. beef back ribs
- Vegetable oil

DRY RUB

- ⅓ cup raw sugar
- 2 Tbsp. kosher salt
- 2 Tbsp. paprika
- 1 Tbsp. black pepper
- 1½ tsp. garlic powder
- 1½ tsp. onion powder
- 1½ tsp. ground cumin
- ½ tsp. dry mustard
- ¼ tsp. cayenne pepper

BARBECUE SAUCE

- ½ cup spicy brown mustard
- ½ cup apple cider vinegar
- ⅓ cup brown sugar, packed
- 6 Tbsp. ketchup
- 3 Tbsp. melted butter
- 3 Tbsp. Worcestershire sauce
- 1 Tbsp. garlic powder

PREP

1. Combine all the dry rub ingredients in a small bowl. Season the ribs with the dry rub and let sit at room temperature while the grill heats.

2. Prepare grill for indirect heat and preheat to low (250 degrees F). Oil the grates with vegetable oil.

3. Place the ribs on the grill, close the lid and grill for 2½ hours, maintaining the temperature. Flip ribs over and grill with the lid closed for 30 minutes.

4. Wrap the ribs in a double layer of heavy-duty foil, sealing the package well. Grill the wrapped ribs for 1 hour.

5. Combine the barbecue sauce ingredients in a saucepan and whisk to combine. Heat over medium until warm, about 4 minutes. Reserve ¾ of the sauce to serve with the ribs.

6. Remove the ribs from the grill and place on a platter or sheet pan. Remove the ribs from the foil and increase the temperature of the grill to medium (400 degrees F). Brush the ribs with some of the rest of the barbecue sauce and place on the grill until nicely charred, 5 to 15 minutes. Flip over, brush with more sauce and grill until nicely charred, 5 to 15 minutes.

7. Serve the ribs with the reserved barbecue sauce.

SERVES 4–6

PILAR'S CARNE ASADA

Inspired by the love of Duke's life, this beloved Latin American dish will take a place of pride at your cookout spread.

PROVISIONS

- 1 cup chopped fresh cilantro leaves
- ⅓ cup olive oil
- ¼ cup San-J reduced sodium gluten free tamari
- ½ cup fresh orange juice (from 1 large orange)
- 4 Tbsp. fresh lime juice (from 2 large limes)
- 4 cloves garlic, grated or minced
- 2 chipotle peppers in adobo sauce, finely minced
- 1 tsp. ground cumin
- 1 tsp. garlic powder
- 1 tsp. onion powder
-   Kosher or fine sea salt
-   Black pepper
- 1 (1½–2 lb.) flank steak
-   Vegetable oil

FOR SERVING, OPTIONAL

-   Corn tortillas
-   Guacamole
-   Pico de gallo
-   Salsa
-   Cilantro
-   Diced onions

PREP

1. In a medium mixing bowl, combine the cilantro, olive oil, tamari, orange juice, lime juice, garlic, chipotles, cumin, garlic and onion powders, 1 tsp. salt and 1 tsp. pepper. Whisk to combine. Reserve ½ cup marinade; cover and refrigerate until serving time.

John Wayne with his wife Pilar and son Ethan on the set of *The Sons of Katie Elder* (1965).

2. Pour the remaining mixture into a large resealable food storage bag. Add the steak, push out the excess air and seal. Flip the bag several times to coat the meat with the marinade. Marinate for 6 to 12 hours in the refrigerator, flipping the bag over occasionally every few hours.

3. Prepare the grill for direct heat and preheat to medium-high. Oil the grates.

4. Remove the steak from the marinade, discarding the marinade. Pat the steak dry and season with salt and pepper on both sides. Grill with the lid closed for 6 minutes per side or until it reaches an internal temperature of 130 degrees F for medium-rare. Remove from the grill and let rest for 10 minutes. Remove the reserved marinade from the refrigerator and let sit while the steak rests.

5. Slice the steak against the grain, pour the reserved marinade over and serve.

SERVES 6

John Wayne and Louis Johnson surveying cattle at their 26 Bar Ranch in Eagar, Arizona, c. 1969. In the 1940s, the property was known as the Milky Way Ranch.

LUCKY TEXAN LONDON BROIL

Good food can make you feel like a million bucks. In terms of flavor, you just hit the grilling jackpot with this can't-miss classic.

PROVISIONS

1 (2–2 ½ lb.) London broil

Vegetable oil

BLUE CHEESE SAUCE

⅔ cup sour cream

⅓ cup mayonnaise

2 tsp. Worcestershire sauce

4 oz. crumbled blue cheese

Kosher or fine sea salt and pepper, to taste

MARINADE

½ cup olive oil

¼ cup soy sauce

¼ cup red wine vinegar

1 Tbsp. Dijon mustard

1 Tbsp. Worcestershire sauce

2 cloves garlic, minced

PREP

1. Combine all the blue cheese sauce ingredients in a mixing bowl. Season to taste with salt and pepper. Cover with plastic wrap and refrigerate until ready to serve.

2. Whisk all the marinade ingredients together in a mixing bowl. Pour the marinade into a plastic food storage bag. Place the London broil in the bag, flipping several times to coat the meat with the marinade. Let sit at room temperature for

Barbara Sheldon, Lloyd Whitlock and John Wayne in *The Lucky Texan* (1934).

30 minutes or refrigerate for up to 24 hours. If marinating in the refrigerator, let sit at room temperature for 20 to 30 minutes before grilling.

3. Prepare the grill for direct heat and preheat to medium-high.

4. Remove the meat from the marinade, discarding the marinade, and pat dry with paper towels.

5. Brush the grates of the grill with oil and grill the meat with the lid open for 6 to 8 minutes per side or until it reaches an internal temperature of 125 degrees F for medium-rare. Place the meat on a cutting board, cover with foil and let sit for 10 minutes before serving. Slice thinly across the grain and serve with the blue cheese sauce.

SERVES 6

THE CONQUEROR'S STEAK KEBABS
WITH TARRAGON AIOLI

When hungry guests are storming to your table by the dozen, take no prisoners with the Genghis Khan of grilled meats—sizzling steak skewers paired with a tangy tarragon and garlic sauce.

PROVISIONS

TARRAGON AIOLI

- ¾ cup mayonnaise
- 2 Tbsp. red wine vinegar
- 2 cloves garlic, minced
- 3 Tbsp. finely chopped fresh tarragon
- ½ tsp. pepper
- Kosher or fine sea salt

KEBABS

- ½ cup olive oil
- ¼ cup red wine vinegar
- 1 tsp. garlic powder
- 1 tsp. onion powder
- ½ tsp. kosher or fine sea salt
- ½ tsp. pepper
- 1½ lb. sirloin, cut into 1½-inch pieces
- 1 lb. white button mushrooms
- 1 green bell pepper, cut into 1-inch chunks
- 1 red bell pepper, cut into 1-inch chunks
- 1 small red onion, cut into wedges

PREP

1. Combine all the tarragon aioli ingredients in a small bowl. Cover and refrigerate until ready to serve.

John Wayne in *The Conqueror* (1956).

2. Combine olive oil, ¼ cup red wine vinegar, garlic and onion powders, ½ tsp. salt and ½ tsp. pepper in a large mixing bowl. Add the cut sirloin and mushrooms and stir to ensure the meat and mushrooms are well coated. Cover bowl with plastic wrap and allow to marinate for 30 minutes at room temperature.

3. Prepare grill for direct heat and preheat to medium-high.

4. Remove meat and mushrooms from the bowl and discard the marinade. Thread the meat, mushrooms, peppers and onions onto six metal skewers, alternating meat and vegetables.

5. Grill with lid closed 2 to 3 minutes on four sides for a total of 8 to 12 minutes.

6. Serve the kebabs with the tarragon sauce.

SERVES 6

GRILLED SIRLOIN
WITH POBLANO PEPPER SAUCE

Part of the joy of cooking for a crowd is knowing food tastes better when you give it the time it deserves by making it yourself. Fortunately, roasting the poblano pepper to make this tempting pepper sauce only takes about 12 minutes. Then you can let a food processor and the grill do the rest.

PROVISIONS

Vegetable oil

1 poblano pepper

2 (1½ lb.) sirloin steaks, ½-inch thick

Olive oil

Montreal steak seasoning (see p. 50)

¾ cup mayonnaise

1 tsp. agave or honey

1 tsp. ground cumin

½ tsp. garlic powder

PREP

1. Prepare grill for direct heat and preheat to medium-high. Oil the grates.

2. Place the poblano pepper on the grill and grill with the lid up until fully charred on all sides, about 5 to 6 minutes per side. Place in a bowl and cover with a plate or plastic wrap and let steam until cool enough to handle.

3. Remove the steaks from the refrigerator, brush both sides with olive oil and season with the steak seasoning. Let sit at room temperature for 20 to 30 minutes.

4. Peel the skin off of the pepper and remove the stem and seeds. Puree in a food processor until smooth. Add the mayonnaise, agave or

John Wayne and the cast of *Fort Apache* (1948).

honey, cumin and garlic powder; blend until smooth.

5. Place the steaks on the grill and grill with the lid closed for 5 minutes per side or until they reach an internal temperature of 130 degrees F for medium rare.

6. Let the steaks rest for 10 minutes. Serve with the sauce.

SERVES 4–6

YAKIMA CANUTT'S PEPPER CRUSTED T-BONE STEAK

Named for the champion cowboy and stuntman Duke met at the beginning of his career, this dish will compel you to develop your own "pass system" at the table—for seconds and thirds, that is!

PROVISIONS

8	Tbsp. butter, room temperature
1	large shallot, minced
4	cloves garlic, minced, divided
¼	cup chopped chives
1	Tbsp. plus ¼ cup Worcestershire sauce, divided
½	cup olive oil
⅓	cup low sodium soy sauce
¼	cup freshly squeezed lemon juice
1	Tbsp. Italian seasoning
1	tsp. black pepper
1	tsp. onion powder
½	tsp. kosher or fine sea salt
4	(10-oz.) T-bone steaks
	Vegetable oil

PREP

1. Melt 1 Tbsp. butter in a small skillet over medium heat. Add the shallots and cook, stirring occasionally, until soft but not browned. Add two cloves of minced garlic and cook for 30 seconds. Place mixture in a small mixing bowl and let cool. Add the remaining butter, chives and 1 Tbsp. Worcestershire sauce. Mix well. Transfer butter mixture to plastic wrap and form butter into a 5-inch long log. Roll up in plastic, enclosing it completely; refrigerate until firm. (Can be prepared 3 days ahead. Keep refrigerated.)

2. Combine the remaining ¼ cup Worcestershire sauce, remaining two minced garlic cloves, olive oil, soy sauce, lemon juice, Italian seasoning, black pepper, onion powder and salt in a mixing bowl and mix well. Pour into a large resealable food storage bag, add the steaks and marinate in the refrigerator for 1 to 24 hours.

3. Remove the steaks from the marinade, pat dry with paper towels and let sit at room temperature while the grill heats.

4. Prepare grill for direct heat and preheat to medium-high. Oil the grates with vegetable oil.

5. Grill the steaks with the lid closed for 5 minutes per side or until they reach an internal temperature of 130 degrees F for medium-rare. Remove from grill and let rest for 5 to 10 minutes.

6. Slice the compound butter into eight slices. Top the warm steaks with two slices of butter per steak and serve.

SERVES 4

CHEESE-AND-RED-PEPPER-STUFFED FLANK STEAK

Packed with two types of cheese and tasty red peppers, this Mediterannean-inspired plate is in an all-in-one meal that tastes even better than it looks, no sides necessary.

PROVISIONS

- 1 (12-oz.) jar roasted red peppers, drained
- ¼ cup olive oil plus more for the outside of the steak
- ¼ cup grated Parmesan cheese
- 2 cloves garlic, chopped
- ½ cup toasted walnut pieces
- 1 cup crumbled feta cheese
- 1 (1½–2 lb.) flank steak
- Everything bagel seasoning
- Vegetable oil

PREP

1. Put the peppers, ¼ cup olive oil, Parmesan, garlic, walnuts and feta cheese in a food processor and process until it creates a thick paste. Remove half to serve with the steak.

2. Place the flank steak on a cutting board with the grain running parallel to the edge of the counter. Place your hand on top of the steak and cut the steak horizontally to but not through the other side. Open the steak up like a book and pound it to an even thickness.

3. Spread half the pepper feta spread across the cut part of the steak leaving a 1-inch border around the edges. Gently roll the steak into a long log, tightening as you go. Place it seam-

Duke sailing aboard the *Wild Goose* off the coast of Cannes in 1963.

side down and tie butcher's twine at 1- to 2-inch intervals. Rub olive oil all over the outside and sprinkle it generously with everything bagel seasoning. Let it rest while the grill heats.

4. Prepare grill for direct and indirect heat and preheat to medium-high. Oil the grates with vegetable oil.

5. Grill the steak over the direct side for 2 to 3 minutes, rotate a quarter turn, grill for 2 to 3 minutes, rotate another quarter turn, grill for 2 to 3 minutes, then grill the final side for 2 to 3 minutes. Transfer to the indirect side of the grill, close the lid and grill for 25 minutes or until it reaches an internal temperature of 140 degrees F for medium. Remove from the grill and let rest for 10 minutes before removing the twine, slicing and serving with the reserved spread.

SERVES 6

BISTECCA ALLA FIORENTINA

The pride of Florence, this sizable Tuscan-style porterhouse has been beloved by red meat connoisseurs for generations. Simply put, it's a thing of butter-brushed beauty.

PROVISIONS

1	Tbsp. kosher salt
1	Tbsp. garlic powder
1½	tsp. black pepper
1	(2½–3 lb.) porterhouse steak
	Olive oil
	Vegetable oil
2	sprigs each fresh rosemary, thyme and sage
3	Tbsp. melted butter
1	lemon

PREP

1. Combine the salt, garlic powder and pepper in a small bowl. Remove the steak from the refrigerator and allow it to sit at room temperature for 1 hour. Brush both sides of the steak with olive oil and season generously with the salt mixture.

2. Prepare the grill for direct heat and preheat to medium high. Oil the grates with vegetable oil.

3. Tie the herbs together at the stem ends with butcher's twine.

4. Grill the steak for 6 minutes with the lid closed. Flip the steak and begin basting by dipping the herbs into the melted butter and brushing the steak with them often. Continue to grill with the lid up for 6 minutes or until the steak reaches an internal temperature of 130 degrees F for medium rare.

5. Squeeze the lemon over the steak and let rest for 10 minutes before carving and slicing the steak.

SERVES 2–3

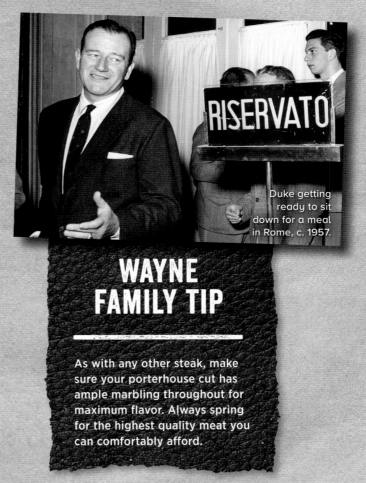

Duke getting ready to sit down for a meal in Rome, c. 1957.

WAYNE FAMILY TIP

As with any other steak, make sure your porterhouse cut has ample marbling throughout for maximum flavor. Always spring for the highest quality meat you can comfortably afford.

All-American Barbecue
Chicken, p. 102

CHICKEN

Whether threaded onto skewers or butterflied on the grill, this lean meat is a chef's blank slate, and the secret's all in the seasoning.

Sweet and Spicy Grilled Chicken Breasts

Sticky-Sweet Grilled Chicken Skewers

Butterflied Chicken on the Grill

Grilled Chicken Paillard with Grilled Corn Salsa

Jerk Chicken Skewers with Honey Lime Sauce

Argentine Chicken Thighs

Arizona Dry-Rubbed Grilled Drumsticks

Country-Style Grilled Lemon Garlic Chicken Leg Quarters

Goat Cheese and Sundried Tomato Chicken Breasts

Tuscan Chicken Under a Brick

All-American Barbecue Chicken

Cliantro Lime Chicken Breasts

Soy Ginger Cedar Plank Chicken Thighs

Comancheros Chicken and Chorizo Skewers

Orange Chipotle Grilled Chicken with Citrus Salsa

Spicy Grilled Chicken Breasts with Alabama White Sauce

Grilled Chicken Breasts with Mango Salsa

John Wayne takes a coffee break during production on *Tall in the Saddle* (1944).

SWEET AND SPICY GRILLED CHICKEN BREASTS

The smell of this dish's heavenly brown sugar spice rub wafting through the house will have the whole family running to the table.

PROVISIONS

SPICE RUB

- 2 Tbsp. brown sugar
- 1 Tbsp. smoked paprika
- 2 tsp. kosher or fine sea salt
- 1 tsp. garlic powder
- 1 tsp. onion powder
- ½ tsp. chipotle chili powder

- 4 bone-in, skin-on chicken breasts
  Olive oil
  Vegetable oil

SAUCE

- 2 Tbsp. butter
- 2 Tbsp. honey
- 1 Tbsp. hot sauce

PREP

1. Combine all rub ingredients in a small bowl.

2. Brush the chicken breasts with olive oil, rub liberally with the spice rub and let sit for 15 minutes at room temperature.

3. Prepare grill for direct and indirect heat and preheat to medium-high.

4. Brush the grill grates with vegetable oil. Place the chicken breasts skin side up on the indirect heat side of the grill, close the lid and grill for 15 minutes. Flip the chicken and grill for 20 minutes or until it reaches an internal temperature of 160 degrees F.

5. While the chicken is grilling, make the sauce by heating the butter, honey and hot sauce in a small saucepan.

6. When the chicken breasts have reached an internal temperature of 160 degrees F, brush them with the sauce, then move them to the direct heat side of the grill and cook for 1 minute. Brush with more sauce, flip and grill for another minute.

7. Remove chicken breasts from grill, brush with more sauce and serve.

SERVES 4

STICKY-SWEET GRILLED CHICKEN SKEWERS

This finger-licking recipe is irresistible, so make sure you double up on the portions before you fire up the grill!

PROVISIONS

- ¾ **cup teriyaki sauce**
- ⅓ **cup apricot preserves**
- ¼ **cup cilantro leaves and stems, coarsely chopped**
- 2 **Tbsp. lime juice**
- 1 **Tbsp. sesame oil**
- 1 **Tbsp. fresh ginger, grated**
- 2 **cloves garlic, minced**
- 1 **small jalapeño pepper, seeded, deveined and minced**
- 2 **lb. boneless, skinless chicken thighs or breasts, cut into bite-size pieces**
- 8 **skewers**

  Fresh cilantro leaves and grated lime zest, for garnish

  Vegetable oil

PREP

1. Stir together the teriyaki sauce, preserves, chopped cilantro, lime juice, sesame oil, ginger, garlic and jalapeño in a medium bowl. Reserve ⅓ cup mixture and store covered in the refrigerator.

2. Place chicken and remaining marinade in a large resealable food storage bag and seal well; refrigerate for 2 hours (or up to 24 hours).

3. Allow reserved marinade to come to room temperature. If using wooden skewers, soak in water for 30 minutes.

4. Remove chicken from bag (discard bag and marinade). Thread chicken onto skewers and cook on a well-oiled grill over medium-high heat for 3 to 4 minutes on each side or until chicken is cooked through. Remove from grill to a platter and drizzle with reserved marinade. Garnish with cilantro and lime zest, if desired.

SERVES 8

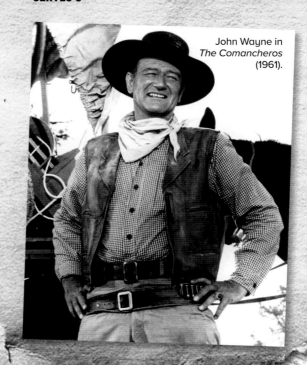

John Wayne in
The Comancheros
(1961).

BUTTERFLIED CHICKEN ON THE GRILL

If you're looking for a lean, mean protein that packs in the flavor, this split bird'll deliver and cooks in a flash.

PROVISIONS

- ½ cup vegetable oil, plus more for the grill
- 2 Tbsp. finely minced garlic
- 2 Tbsp. fresh thyme leaves, finely chopped
- 3 whole lemons
- 2 tsp. kosher or fine sea salt
- 1 tsp. black pepper
- 1 tsp. onion powder
- 1 (3-lb.) whole chicken, butterflied

Duke reads to his children, Patrick, Melinda, Toni and Michael, 1942.

PREP

1. Combine the oil, garlic and thyme leaves in a large baking dish. Zest and juice one lemon and add to the mixture along with the salt, pepper and onion powder. Mix well. Add the chicken, turn to coat, cover and refrigerate for 2 to 8 hours.

2. Prepare grill for direct and indirect heat and preheat to medium. Brush the grates with oil.

3. Remove the chicken from the marinade, place skin side down on the grill over direct heat. Grill for 15 minutes or until the skin is golden and crispy. Flip and grill over direct heat for 4 to 5 minutes, move to the indirect side of the grill, cover the grill and cook for another 15 minutes or until the chicken reaches an internal temperature of 160 degrees F. Remove from the grill, cover loosely with foil and let rest for 10 minutes.

4. Cut the remaining two lemons in half and grill flesh side down until charred, about 5 minutes. Serve the charred lemons with the chicken.

SERVES 4

WAYNE FAMILY TIP

You can take Duke's lead and support small businesses by having your local butcher butterfly your meat for you.

GRILLED CHICKEN PAILLARD
WITH GRILLED CORN SALSA

"Paillard" (pronounced pie-YAHRD) might as well be French for "roll up your sleeves," so grab a mallet and go to town before you throw this bird on the grill!

PROVISIONS

- 4 boneless, skinless chicken breast halves
- ¼ cup olive oil
- Juice of 3 limes, divided
- 1 small shallot, minced
- Black pepper
- Kosher or fine sea salt
- 2 ears of corn, shucked and silk removed
- 2 medium tomatoes, diced
- ¼ medium red onion, diced
- 1 jalapeño or serrano pepper, seeded, deveined and finely minced
- ⅓ cup fresh cilantro leaves, chopped
- Vegetable oil

John Wayne and Joan Crawford in *Reunion in France* (1942).

PREP

1. Place each chicken breast half between two sheets of waxed paper and pound with a meat mallet, rolling pin or heavy pan until about ¼-inch thick. Place the chicken halves in a large baking dish.

2. In a small bowl, whisk together the olive oil, juice of two limes, shallot and ¼ tsp. of pepper. Pour the mixture over the chicken. Flip the chicken to coat, cover and refrigerate for 30 minutes.

3. Prepare grill for direct heat and preheat to high.

4. Oil the grates. Grill the corn, turning often, for 10 minutes or until charred all over. Let cool to the touch. Slice off the kernels and place in a mixing bowl. Add the tomato, onion, jalapeño or serrano pepper, juice of 1 lime, cilantro and salt and pepper to taste. Stir to combine and let sit at room temperature until the chicken is ready.

5. Remove the chicken from the marinade and discard the marinade. Pat dry, then sprinkle with salt on both sides. Grill for 2 to 3 minutes per side or until golden brown and the juices run clear.

6. Serve the chicken topped with the salsa.

SERVES 4

JERK CHICKEN SKEWERS
WITH HONEY LIME SAUCE

This Jamaican-style chicken will set your taste buds on fire in the best way possible.

PROVISIONS

6	(approximately 6 oz. each) boneless, skinless chicken breast halves
1	habanero or Scotch bonnet chili pepper
1	cup fresh cilantro leaves
½	cup olive or vegetable oil
4	green onions, white and light green parts, chopped
6	peeled garlic cloves
2	Tbsp. sugar
1	Tbsp. ground allspice
1	Tbsp. dried ginger
2	limes, divided
	Kosher or fine sea salt
	Black pepper
½	cup sour cream
1	Tbsp. honey
12	skewers

PREP

1. Cut the chicken lengthwise into even strips, ½- to ¾-inch thick. Place in a large food storage bag.

2. Wearing gloves, remove the stem, seeds and veins from the chili pepper and place in a small food processor or blender. Add the cilantro, oil, green onions, garlic, sugar, allspice, ginger, juice of one lime, 2 tsp. salt and 1 tsp. pepper. Process into a thick paste, then pour into the bag. Seal the bag and mix well to fully coat the chicken with the jerk paste. Refrigerate for at least 1 hour or up to 8 hours.

3. Combine the sour cream with the finely grated zest and juice of one lime and the honey. Cover and refrigerate until serving time. If using wooden skewers, soak them for 30 minutes in water. Prepare grill for direct heat and preheat to high (450–550 degrees F).

4. Wearing gloves, thread the chicken onto skewers and let sit at room temperature while the grill preheats.

5. Oil the grates of the grill. Cook the skewers over direct heat with the lid closed for 6 to 8 minutes or until the chicken reaches an internal temperature of 165 degrees F, turning once or twice while cooking. Serve with the sauce on the side.

SERVES 6

John Wayne in *Brannigan* (1975).

ARGENTINE CHICKEN THIGHS

The chimichurri marinade on this platter might hail from the "land of silver," but it'll be the new gold standard when it comes to elevating your grilling game.

PROVISIONS

1	cup Italian parsley
¼	cup cilantro leaves
½	cup olive oil
¼	cup white wine vinegar
1	tsp. dried oregano
1	tsp. kosher or fine sea salt
½	tsp. pepper
½	tsp. red pepper flakes
8	boneless, skinless chicken thighs
	Vegetable oil

PREP

1. Place the parsley, cilantro, olive oil, vinegar, oregano, salt, pepper and red pepper in a blender and process until well blended, scraping down the sides as needed. Reserve ½ cup of the mixture in a covered container and refrigerate until serving time. Pour the rest into a large food storage bag and add the chicken thighs. Squeeze out the excess air, seal the bag and refrigerate for 1 to 12 hours.

2. Prepare grill for direct heat and preheat to medium-high.

3. Remove the chicken from the bag, discarding any marinade. Brush the grill grates with vegetable oil and grill chicken 4 to 5 minutes per side or until the internal temperature reaches 160 to 165 degrees F.

4. Serve the chicken with the reserved sauce.

SERVES 4

John Wayne, Edwin L. Marin and Earl McKee on the set of *Tall in the Saddle* (1944).

AMERICAN GRILL FACTS

According to the National Chicken Council, in 2018, Americans consumed more than 93.5 pounds of chicken per capita.

ARIZONA DRY-RUBBED GRILLED DRUMSTICKS

You don't necessarily need sauce to feel the desert heat.

PROVISIONS

- 2 **Tbsp. garlic powder**
- 2 **Tbsp. onion powder**
- 2 **Tbsp. brown sugar**
- 2 **tsp. paprika**
- 1 **tsp. chili powder**
- ½ **tsp. kosher or fine sea salt**
- ¼ **tsp. black pepper**
- 8 **chicken drumsticks**
- **Vegetable oil**

PREP

1. Prepare grill for direct heat and preheat to medium-high (425 degrees F).

2. Combine the garlic and onion powders, brown sugar, paprika, chili powder, salt and pepper and fully coat the drumsticks with the dry rub.

3. Oil the grill grates and grill for 15 to 20 minutes or until the internal temperature reaches 165 degrees F. Turn the drumsticks every 5 minutes. Let rest for 5 minutes before serving.

SERVES 4

John Wayne and Shirley Jean Rickert in '*Neath the Arizona Skies* (1934).

WAYNE FAMILY TIP

If you and yours share Duke's love of spicy food, dial up the flavor by adding a generous pinch of cayenne pepper to your dry rub mix.

Duke at the Black Lake Hunting & Fishing Club in Campti, Louisiana. The icon spent time in the Bayou State while filming *The Horse Soldiers* (1959).

John Ford, Constance Towers and John Wayne on the set of *The Horse Soldiers* (1959).

COUNTRY-STYLE GRILLED LEMON GARLIC CHICKEN LEG QUARTERS

Much like John Wayne and his mentor, John Ford, lemon and garlic is a perfect pairing—and in this case, it makes for an unforgettable meal.

PROVISIONS

½ cup olive oil

¼ cup plus 1 Tbsp. lemon juice, divided

2 garlic cloves, minced or grated

1 tsp. paprika

1 tsp. dried thyme

Kosher or fine sea salt

Pepper

4 whole chicken leg quarters, bone-in, skin-on

Vegetable oil

1 Tbsp. butter

1 Tbsp. flour

1 cup chicken broth

Chopped parsley, for garnish

PREP

1. Combine olive oil, ¼ cup lemon juice, garlic, paprika, thyme, 1 tsp. salt and ½ tsp. pepper. Place the chicken legs in a dish that will fit the pieces in a single layer and add the marinade. Flip chicken pieces to coat well. Cover and refrigerate for 1 hour or up to 8 hours. Remove chicken from refrigerator and let stand at room temperature while the grill heats.

2. Prepare grill for direct and indirect heat and preheat to medium (about 350 degrees F). Oil the grates with vegetable oil.

3. Place the chicken over direct heat for 2 to 3 minutes per side to sear. Move to the indirect heat side, close the lid and grill for 35 to 45 minutes or until the chicken reaches an internal temperature of 165 degrees F, flipping every 8 to 10 minutes.

4. Melt the butter over medium heat in a saucepan either on the burner of the grill or on the stove. Whisk in the flour and let cook, whisking for 1 minute. Add the chicken broth and 1 Tbsp. lemon juice and cook, stirring occasionally, until thickened, about 5 minutes. Season to taste with salt and pepper.

5. Place the chicken legs on a platter, spoon on the sauce and garnish with parsley.

SERVES 4

GOAT CHEESE AND SUNDRIED TOMATO CHICKEN BREASTS

Rich, flavorful ingredients like goat cheese and sundried tomatoes turn this humble grilled dish into a 5-star affair.

PROVISIONS

4	chicken breast halves
	Kosher or fine sea salt
	Pepper
¼	cup sundried tomato pesto
8	oz. goat cheese
12	fresh basil leaves
	Olive oil
	Vegetable oil
	Balsamic glaze

PREP

1. Prepare grill for direct heat and preheat to medium to medium-high (about 400 degrees F).

2. Place the chicken breasts between two pieces of waxed paper and pound thin with a mallet or rolling pin.

3. Salt and pepper the inside of each breast. Spread a layer of pesto on each and divide the goat cheese among the breasts, keeping a little border. Top each breast with three basil leaves. Roll the breasts up and tie with chicken string or secure with toothpicks. Brush the outside of the chicken with olive oil and sprinkle with salt and pepper.

4. Oil the grill grates. Place the chicken on the grates and grill for 8 to 12 minutes (depending on thickness), flipping every few minutes to ensure the chicken is browned all over.

5. When the chicken reaches an internal temperature of 165 degrees F, remove from the grill and let sit for 5 minutes. Slice and serve with a drizzle of balsamic glaze.

SERVES 4

John Wayne in *North to Alaska* (1960).

DID YOU KNOW?

North to Alaska (1960) was the third of six films John Wayne made with director Henry Hathaway, which ended with *True Grit* (1969).

TUSCAN CHICKEN UNDER A BRICK

Duke was no stranger to Italy's charms. Also known as *pollo al mattone*, this innovative meal makes use of heated bricks to ensure a delightfully crispy crust every time.

PROVISIONS

1	garlic clove
2	Tbsp. kosher or fine sea salt
1	Tbsp. fresh rosemary
2	tsp. black pepper
1	tsp. dried oregano
¼	tsp. crushed red pepper flakes
	Finely grated zest of 1 lemon
4	bone-in, skin-on chicken breasts, ribs removed
	Olive oil
	Vegetable oil
2	whole lemons
4	bricks

PREP

1. Combine the garlic, salt, rosemary, pepper, oregano, red pepper flakes and lemon zest in a spice grinder or food processor and process until fully combined and finely chopped.

2. Pat chicken breasts dry, brush with olive oil, then spread the seasoning on both sides of the chicken breasts. Let sit at room temperature while preheating the grill.

3. Prepare the grill for direct and indirect heat. Wrap four bricks with heavy duty aluminum foil and place over direct heat. Preheat grill to medium (350 degrees F).

4. Oil the grill grates. Place each chicken breast skin side down over direct heat and top with a brick. Close the lid and grill for 8 to 10 minutes. Carefully remove the bricks, flip the chicken over and move to the indirect side of the grill. Flip the bricks over and place on top of the chicken. Close the lid and grill for another 10 to 15 minutes or until the chicken reaches an internal temperature of 165 degrees F. During the last 5 minutes of grilling, cut the lemons in half and place cut side down over direct heat.

5. Serve the grilled lemon halves with the chicken.

SERVES 4

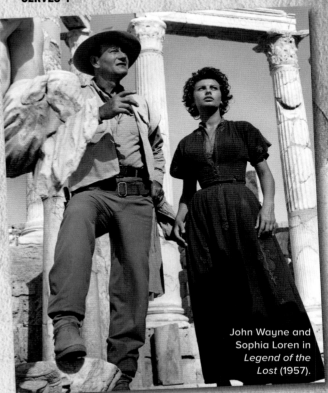

John Wayne and Sophia Loren in *Legend of the Lost* (1957).

ALL-AMERICAN BARBECUE CHICKEN

Every respectable grillmaster has at least one flawless recipe up their sleeve, and pilgrim, this stick-to-your-ribs summertime favorite is your ace in the hole.

PROVISIONS

3	Tbsp. melted butter
¼	cup plus 3 Tbsp. Worcestershire sauce, divided
1	(3 ½-4 lb.) chicken, cut into 8 pieces
	Kosher or fine sea salt
	Pepper
	Vegetable oil
1	cup ketchup
½	cup brown sugar
½	cup honey
¼	cup apple cider vinegar
1 ½	tsp. garlic powder
1 ½	tsp. onion powder

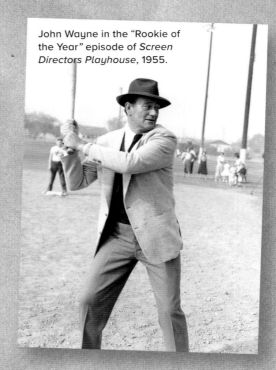

John Wayne in the "Rookie of the Year" episode of *Screen Directors Playhouse*, 1955.

PREP

1. Prepare the grill for direct and indirect heat and preheat to medium.

2. Combine the melted butter with 3 Tbsp. Worcestershire sauce and brush liberally on all sides of the chicken pieces. Season well with salt and pepper. Brush the grill grates with oil.

3. Place the chicken pieces skin side up on the indirect side of the grill placing the smaller pieces farthest away from the heat source. Grill for 20 minutes with the lid closed. Flip the chicken pieces, close the lid and grill for another 20 minutes or until the internal temperature reaches 160 degrees F.

4. Meanwhile, combine the ketchup, brown sugar, honey, remaining ¼ cup Worcestershire sauce, apple cider vinegar, garlic powder and onion powder in a small saucepan. Bring to a boil over medium-high heat, reduce heat and simmer for 10 minutes. Let cool.

5. When the chicken reaches an internal temperature of 160 degrees F, brush with the sauce and move to the direct heat side of the grill. Cook for 4 to 5 more minutes. Brush with sauce and flip every minute or two. Serve any remaining sauce on the side.

SERVES 4-6

John Wayne in *Flame of Barbary Coast* (1945). The film was nominated for two Academy Awards: Best Sound and Best Music Score.

CILANTRO LIME CHICKEN BREASTS

You can always count on chopped jalapeño to kick things up
a notch, especially in this can't-miss citrus-marinated chicken.

PROVISIONS

4	boneless, skinless chicken breasts
1	cup cilantro
½	cup olive oil
1	jalapeño pepper, seeded, deveined and roughly chopped
4	Tbsp. fresh lime juice (from 2 limes)
1	Tbsp. honey
1	tsp. kosher or fine sea salt
½	tsp. pepper
1	tsp. ground cumin
	Vegetable oil
	Lime wedges, for serving

PREP

1. Place each chicken breast between two pieces of waxed paper on a work surface. Using a mallet or rolling pin, pound each chicken breast until it is about ½-inch thick. Place the chicken breasts in a 9- by 12-inch baking dish.

2. Place the cilantro, olive oil, jalapeño, lime juice, honey, salt, pepper and cumin in a blender and process until smooth. Reserve a quarter of the marinade and pour the rest over the chicken breasts, making sure to coat each one well on both sides. Cover with plastic wrap and refrigerate for 30 minutes to 12 hours.

3. Prepare the grill for direct heat and preheat to medium-high.

4. Remove the chicken from the dish and discard the marinade. Brush the grill grates with vegetable oil and grill 3 minutes per side or until the internal temperature reaches 160 to 165 degrees F. Remove the chicken from the grill and immediately brush with the reserved marinade.

5. Serve with lime wedges if desired.

SERVES 4

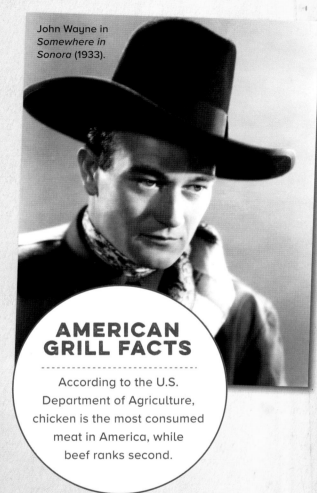

John Wayne in *Somewhere in Sonora* (1933).

AMERICAN GRILL FACTS

According to the U.S. Department of Agriculture, chicken is the most consumed meat in America, while beef ranks second.

SOY GINGER CEDAR PLANK CHICKEN THIGHS

Tip your hat to the flavors of the Far East with this fragrant Asian-inspired dish that tastes out of this world.

PROVISIONS

2	cedar planks
½	cup soy sauce
½	cup balsamic vinegar
½	cup brown sugar
1	Tbsp. finely minced garlic
¼	cup honey
2	Tbsp. sesame oil
2	Tbsp. grated fresh ginger
¾	tsp. red pepper flakes
8	boneless, skinless chicken thighs
1	Tbsp. white sesame seeds

PREP

1. Soak the cedar planks in water for at least 1 hour.

2. In a deep saucepan, combine the soy sauce, vinegar, brown sugar and garlic. Bring to a boil, then lower the heat and gently simmer, stirring occasionally, until reduced by half and thick, about 15 minutes. Remove from the heat, then stir in the honey, sesame oil, ginger and red pepper flakes. Let cool for a few minutes. Reserve ½ cup marinade for later.

3. Put the chicken thighs in a mixing bowl or baking pan and cover with the marinade, making sure the thighs are submerged as much as possible. Refrigerate until time to grill.

4. Prepare grill for direct and indirect heat and preheat to medium (about 400 degrees F).

5. Place the cedar planks over direct heat, close the lid and grill them for 10 minutes or until they start to smoke. Flip them over and place on the indirect side of the grill. Put four chicken thighs on each plank and discard the marinade. Cover the grill and cook for 15 minutes. Cook for another 15 minutes or until the chicken reaches an internal temperature of 165 degrees F, glazing every few minutes with reserved ½ cup marinade.

6. Sprinkle with sesame seeds and serve.

SERVES 4

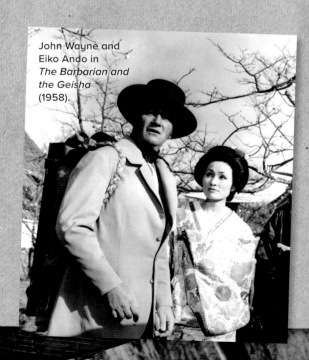

John Wayne and Eiko Ando in *The Barbarian and the Geisha* (1958).

COMANCHEROS CHICKEN AND CHORIZO SKEWERS

When you've got a hard day's work ahead, this spicy, hearty dish delivers double the fuel.

PROVISIONS

20-24	wooden skewers
4	Tbsp. olive oil
2	Tbsp. lemon juice
2	garlic cloves, minced
2	tsp. paprika
1	tsp. kosher or fine sea salt
½	tsp. pepper
2	lb. boneless, skinless chicken thighs, cut into 1-inch pieces
2	lb. Spanish or Portuguese chorizo
2	white onions
	Vegetable oil
2	cups arugula
2	lemons, cut into wedges for serving

John Wayne and Stuart Whitman in *The Comancheros* (1961).

AMERICAN GRILL FACTS

There are two types of chorizo: Spanish and Mexican. In the U.S., Spanish chorizo is sold either dry (and will need to be sliced like pepperoni) or soft (a.k.a. semi-cured).

PREP

1. Soak the skewers in water for 30 minutes.

2. Combine the olive oil, lemon juice, garlic, paprika, salt and pepper in a mixing bowl. Add the cut up chicken thighs, toss to coat and let marinate for 15 to 20 minutes.

3. Prepare the grill for direct heat and preheat to medium-high.

4. Slice the chorizo into ¼-inch rounds.

5. Cut the onions in half horizontally, then cut each half into six wedges.

6. Alternate chorizo, chicken and a few slices of onion on the skewers, thread about 4 of each on each skewer. Brush the grill grates with vegetable oil and grill 8 to 10 minutes with the lid closed, turning the skewers every 2 minutes.

7. Serve the skewers on a bed of arugula with lemon wedges.

MAKES 20–24 SKEWERS

ORANGE CHIPOTLE GRILLED CHICKEN
WITH CITRUS SALSA

Much like a summer sunset, this delicious dish will linger in your mind long after the last bite.

PROVISIONS

- ½ **cup orange marmalade**
- ½ **cup olive oil**
- 1 **tsp. kosher salt**
- ½ **tsp. freshly ground black pepper**
- 1¼-½ **tsp. chipotle chili powder, divided**
- 12 **boneless, skinless chicken thighs, trimmed of any excess fat**
- 3 **medium oranges, peeled and chopped**
- ½ **medium red onion, diced**
- 2 **plum tomatoes, seeded and chopped**
- ¼ **cup fresh cilantro, roughly chopped**
- **Juice of 1 lime**
- **Vegetable oil**

PREP

1. In a small mixing bowl, whisk together the marmalade, olive oil, salt, pepper and 1 tsp. chipotle chili powder. Pour the mixture into a large food storage bag. Add the chicken thighs and marinate at room temperature for 1 hour or overnight in the refrigerator.

2. In a medium mixing bowl, combine the chopped oranges, red onion, tomatoes, cilantro, lime juice and ¼-½ tsp. chipotle chili powder (depending on your preference for spice). Set aside.

3. Heat grill to medium-high and brush the grates with oil. Remove the chicken from the marinade and discard the marinade. Pat the chicken dry and grill covered for 6 to 8 minutes per side.

4. Serve with the citrus salsa.

SERVES 6

Duke with his son Ethan on a toy horse in an undated photo.

DID YOU KNOW?

During Duke's childhood, when the Morrison family lived in Lancaster, California, the legend had a mare named Jenny that he rode to and from school.

SPICY GRILLED CHICKEN BREASTS
WITH ALABAMA WHITE SAUCE

This savory white BBQ sauce will cement your status as the reigning champ of the neighborhood cookout.

PROVISIONS

DRY RUB

2	Tbsp. chili powder
2	tsp. kosher or fine sea salt
2	tsp. garlic powder
1 ½	tsp. cayenne pepper
1	tsp. pepper
½	tsp. dried cumin
	Olive oil
6	bone-in, skin on chicken breasts

ALABAMA WHITE SAUCE

1	cup mayonnaise
2	Tbsp. apple cider vinegar
1	Tbsp. prepared horseradish
2	tsp. sugar
1	tsp. kosher or fine sea salt
½	tsp. pepper
	Vegetable oil

John Wayne in *Trouble Along the Way* (1953).

PREP

1. Combine all rub ingredients together in a small bowl.

2. Brush the chicken wings with olive oil and liberally season with the dry rub. Place chicken in a large food storage bag, squeeze out excess air, seal and refrigerate for 1 to 12 hours.

3. Whisk all sauce ingredients together in a small mixing bowl. Cover with plastic wrap and refrigerate until ready to serve. (Can be prepared up to 3 days in advance.)

4. Prepare the grill for indirect heat and preheat to medium. Brush the grill grates with oil. Place the chicken on the grill skin side down, close the lid and grill for 15 minutes. Flip the chicken over, close the lid and grill for another 15 to 20 minutes or until the chicken reaches an internal temperature of 165 degrees F.

5. Serve the chicken with the sauce.

SERVES 6

GRILLED CHICKEN BREASTS
WITH MANGO SALSA

This bright mango salsa looks like a fiesta on a plate and tastes like heaven.

PROVISIONS

DRY RUB

2	tsp. chili powder
1	tsp. ground cumin
1	tsp. kosher or fine sea salt
½	tsp. pepper
½	tsp. cayenne pepper
¼	tsp. garlic powder
¼	tsp. onion powder
	Olive oil
4	boneless, skinless chicken breasts

MANGO SALSA

2	ripe mangos, chopped
½	small red onion, finely diced
½	cup fresh cilantro
1	small jalapeño pepper, seeded deveined and minced
4	Tbsp. lime juice (from 2 limes)
	Vegetable oil

PREP

1. Prepare the grill for direct heat and preheat to medium-high.

2. Combine all the rub ingredients together in a small bowl. Brush the chicken breasts with olive oil and apply the rub liberally on all sides. (Can be grilled immediately or covered and placed in the refrigerator for up to 12 hours.)

3. Combine all the salsa ingredients together in a small bowl. Cover with plastic wrap and refrigerate until serving time. (Can be made a day ahead.)

4. Brush the grill grates with oil and grill with the lid closed for 6 to 8 minutes per side or until the chicken reaches an internal temperature of 165 degrees F.

5. Serve the chicken breasts with the salsa.

SERVES 4

Ed Faulkner and John Wayne in *The Green Berets* (1968).

Grilled Salmon Fillets with
Garlic Yogurt Sauce, p. 134

FISH

Take a note from Duke's book and heed the call of the sea with any of these tasty recipes featuring the catch of the day.

Grilled Fish with Brazilian Salsa

Hawaiian Mahi Mahi with Coconut Mango Salsa

Pacific Swordfish Fillets with Herb Citrus Crust

West Coast Halibut with Citrus Salsa

Lemon Spiced Salmon Kabobs

Southwest Grilled Whole Fish with Salsa Verde

Grilled Salmon Fillets with Garlic Yogurt Sauce

Upscale Tuna Salad Niçoise

Grilled Tilapia and Pesto Vegetables

Red Witch Tilapia Tacos with Cherry Chipotle Salsa

Blackened Grouper Sandwiches

Mexican-Style Whole Fish Stuffed with Cilantro and Lime

Duke and Pilar enjoy time in Hawaii in an undated photo.

GRILLED FISH
WITH BRAZILIAN SALSA

Also known as *molho à campanha*, the Brazilian vinaigrette salsa with this fish is the South American answer to Mexico's pico de gallo. It pairs perfectly with any type of grilled meat, but it's particularly stellar with fish.

PROVISIONS

- **1** large ripe tomato, seeded and diced
- **1½** tsp. kosher or fine sea salt, divided
- **½** large red onion, diced
- **1** red or green bell pepper, seeded, deveined and diced
- **1** Fresno or jalapeño pepper, seeded, deveined and finely minced (optional)
- **¼** cup coarsely chopped fresh cilantro, Italian parsley or a combination of both
- **4** Tbsp. rice vinegar, divided
- **4** Tbsp. olive oil, divided
- **¼** tsp. black pepper
- **1** garlic clove, peeled and thinly sliced
- **2** (1- to 1½-lb.) whole fish, such as snapper, trout or branzini

PREP

SALSA

1. Season the tomatoes with 1 tsp. salt and toss to combine. Transfer to a fine mesh sieve or colander and let rest for 15 to 20 minutes to drain. Discard any liquid.

2. Combine the tomatoes with the onion, peppers, cilantro, 2 Tbsp. vinegar and 1 Tbsp. oil, then season to taste with salt and pepper. Let sit at room temperature for 30 minutes or cover and refrigerate for up to 2 days. Let come to room temperature before serving.

FISH

1. In a small saucepan, combine the remaining oil with the garlic on low heat for 2 to 3 minutes or until the garlic barely starts to brown. Remove from the heat, then stir in the remaining vinegar, ½ tsp. salt and ¼ tsp. pepper.

2. Heat grill to medium heat (about 350 degrees F) and brush the grates well with oil.

3. Cut deep slits into each side of the fish, then brush with the garlic mixture in the cavity and outside on both sides. Place the fish on the grill and cook, basting occasionally, until you can easily remove it from the grates without it sticking, about 5 minutes. Flip and grill for another 3 to 5 minutes, again basting occasionally, or until the fish is cooked through and can be easily removed from the grill. Serve with the salsa.

SERVES 4

HAWAIIAN MAHI MAHI
WITH COCONUT MANGO SALSA

This flavorful ode to the Aloha State comes with a little kick courtesy of the minced jalapeño, just the way Duke would've liked it.

PROVISIONS

- ¼ cup light coconut milk
- 8 Tbsp. fresh lime juice (from about 4 or 5 large limes), divided
- 4 (6-oz) mahi mahi fillets
- Olive oil
- 1½ cups diced mango
- 1 red bell pepper, diced
- ½ cup diced red onion
- 1 jalapeño pepper, minced
- ¼ cup chopped cilantro leaves
- Kosher or fine sea salt
- Black pepper
- Vegetable oil for the grill

John Wayne in *Donovan's Reef* (1963).

PREP

1. Combine coconut milk and 4 Tbsp. lime juice in a shallow dish or baking dish. Add the mahi mahi and let marinate at room temperature while the grill is heating, flipping the fillets over a few times.

2. Prepare the grill for direct heat and preheat to medium-high.

3. Combine the mango with the red pepper, onion, jalapeño, cilantro and remaining lime juice. Season to taste with salt and pepper. Set aside.

4. Remove the fish from the marinade and blot dry with a paper towel. Brush both sides with olive oil and season with salt and pepper.

5. Brush the grill grates with vegetable oil. Grill the fish for 4 to 5 minutes or until it releases easily from the grill. Flip and grill for another 3 to 4 minutes or until cooked through. Serve with the mango salsa.

SERVES 4

PACIFIC SWORDFISH FILLETS
WITH HERB CITRUS CRUST

These tasty, meaty swordfish fillets will have even the most stubborn seafood skeptics demanding seconds and thirds.

PROVISIONS

- ½ cup soft herbs (such as basil, parsley, thyme, oregano, mint) measured then minced
- ½ tsp. kosher or fine sea salt
- ¼ tsp. black pepper
- 1 lemon, zest finely grated and juiced
- 2 Tbsp. olive oil
- 2 (approximately 10-oz.) swordfish fillets, ¾-inch thick

  Vegetable oil for the grill

PREP

1. Mix together the herbs, salt, pepper, lemon zest and olive oil.

2. Pat the swordfish dry, then generously brush both sides with the herb mixture. Let sit at room temperature while the grill heats.

3. Prepare grill for direct and indirect heat and preheat to medium. Oil the grill grates.

4. Place the swordfish on the indirect side of the grill and cook, covered, for 4 minutes. Flip and cook, covered, for another 4 minutes. Move to the direct heat side, cook on one side, uncovered, for 1 minute, then flip and cook on the other side for 1 minute or until the fillets have nice grill marks and flake easily.

5. Pour the lemon juice over the fish and serve.

SERVES 2

NOTE Due to this fish's high mercury levels, the FDA recommends pregnant women, young children and women of childbearing age avoid eating swordfish.

John Wayne in *Operation Pacific* (1951).

DID YOU KNOW?

Filmed on location in Hawaii, *Operation Pacific* (1951) featured action scenes that incorporated real footage of fighting during World War II.

WEST COAST HALIBUT
WITH CITRUS SALSA

If you love fishing like Duke, you'll know the only way to make this sweet and spicy dish taste better is to catch it yourself.

PROVISIONS

1   red grapefruit

1   seedless orange

2   tangerines

    Juice of 1 lime

¼   cup finely chopped red onion

1   Fresno chile, seeded, deveined and minced

½   cup fresh cilantro, chopped

    Kosher or fine sea salt

    Black pepper

    Olive oil

4   halibut (or other firm white fish) fillets, ½-¾ inch thick

2   tsp. smoked paprika

    Vegetable oil for the grill

Albert Dekker, John Wayne and Harry Shannon in *In Old California* (1942).

PREP

1. Stand the grapefruit upright and use a thin knife to remove peel and pith in sections, cutting down sides from top to bottom. Then, cut along either side of the membranes to release segments. Chop the segments and place in a medium mixing bowl. Squeeze any juices from the membranes on top. Peel and chop the orange and tangerines. Add the lime juice, onion, chile and cilantro, and stir. Add salt and pepper to taste. Set aside until serving time.

2. Prepare grill for direct heat and preheat to medium-high. Brush the fillets with olive oil. Sprinkle the paprika on both sides of the fillets and season with salt and pepper.

3. Oil the grill grates. Grill the fillets directly over the flame for 4 minutes or until the fish releases from the grates. Flip and grill for another 4 minutes or until the fish is cooked through. Serve with the salsa.

SERVES 4

LEMON SPICED SALMON KABOBS

The Mediterranean-inspired four-spice mix on these grilled-to-perfection salmon kabobs is your new secret seasoning to just about any grilled fish.

PROVISIONS

- 1 Tbsp. fresh thyme leaves, chopped
- 1 tsp. ground cumin
- 1 tsp. hot paprika
- 1 tsp. kosher or fine sea salt
- ¼ tsp. crushed red pepper flakes
- 1½ lb. skinless salmon fillet, cut into 1-inch pieces
- 2 organic lemons, thinly sliced, seeds removed
- 16 wooden skewers, soaked in water for 1 hour
- 2 Tbsp. olive oil
- Vegetable oil for the grill

PREP

1. Combine the thyme, cumin, paprika, salt and red pepper flakes in a small bowl and set aside.

2. Prepare the grill for direct heat and preheat to medium-high.

3. Starting and ending with salmon, thread the salmon and lemon slices folded in half onto two skewers, making a total of eight kabobs.

4. Brush the skewers with olive oil and sprinkle the spice mix evenly on all sides of the skewers.

5. Brush the grates with vegetable oil. Grill over direct heat, turning occasionally, until the salmon is opaque, 5 to 8 minutes. Serve.

MAKES 8 SKEWERS

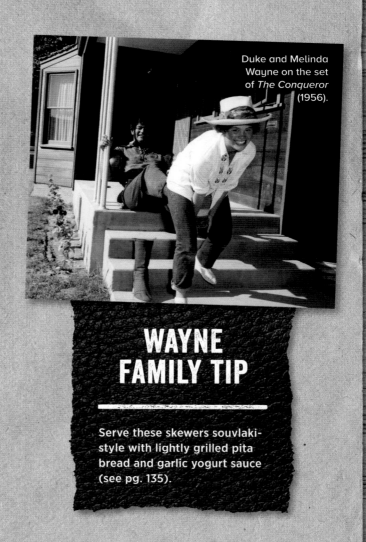

Duke and Melinda Wayne on the set of *The Conqueror* (1956).

WAYNE FAMILY TIP

Serve these skewers souvlaki-style with lightly grilled pita bread and garlic yogurt sauce (see pg. 135).

SOUTHWEST GRILLED WHOLE FISH
WITH SALSA VERDE

Capers and anchovies elevate this salsa verde fish to a whole new level of succulent savory goodness.

PROVISIONS

- 2 **cups fresh soft herbs (such as parsley, basil, mint, thyme and oregano), measured then minced**
- 2 **cloves garlic, finely grated or minced**
- 1 **Tbsp. capers in brine, drained**
- 2 **anchovy fillets in oil**
- ¼ **tsp. crushed red pepper flakes**
- 2 **lemons, plus more for serving**
- ½ **cup olive oil plus more for preparing the fish**
- **Kosher or fine sea salt**
- **Black pepper**
- 1 **(approximately 3-lb.) whole fish such as red snapper, sea bass or branzino, cleaned and scaled**
- **Vegetable oil**

Henry Fonda, Engineer Tom Gray, John Ford and John Wayne during filming of *Fort Apache* (1948).

PREP

1. Combine the herbs, garlic, capers, anchovies and red pepper flakes in a small mixing bowl. Stir with a fork, smashing the anchovies with the back of the fork to break them down and fully incorporate them into the mixture (or you can use a small food processor). Cut the lemons in half, then slice one of the lemon halves and reserve. Juice the other 1½ lemons and add to the herb mixture. Whisk in the olive oil; taste and add salt and pepper if needed.

2. Using kitchen shears, cut the fins off the fish. Rinse and dry the fish, inside and out. Using a sharp knife cut three to four deep slits into the flesh of the fish. Brush the fish inside and out with some of the salsa verde, making sure to get some in each of the slits. Place the reserved lemon slices in the cavity of the fish and let sit at room temperature while the grill heats up.

3. Prepare the grill for direct heat and preheat to medium-high. If using a grill basket (recommended), oil it well inside and out. If not using a grill basket, make sure the grates are very clean and well oiled to keep the fish from sticking.

4. Grill the fish for 8 to 10 minutes per side or until the flesh just flakes with a fork.

5. Drizzle the fish with some of the salsa verde and serve the rest on the side.

SERVES 4

Duke enjoys a day at sea aboard the *Wild Goose* in June, 1967. The legend spent a great deal of his free time aboard the yacht, sailing to Mexico and various ports along the Pacific coast.

GRILLED SALMON FILLETS
WITH GARLIC YOGURT SAUCE

The creamy Greek yogurt sauce with these salmon fillets isn't just incredibly delicious and easy to whip up—it's good for you, pilgrim!

PROVISIONS

- 1 jalapeño pepper, seeded and deveined, roughly chopped
- 2 garlic cloves
- Kosher or fine sea salt
- 1 cup fresh cilantro leaves
- ½ cup full-fat Greek yogurt
- Juice of 1 lime
- 4 (6–8 oz.) skin-on salmon fillets
- Olive oil
- Pepper
- Vegetable oil for the grill

PREP

1. Combine the jalapeño pepper and garlic cloves with ¾ tsp. salt in a small food processor or blender and pulse several times. Add the cilantro, pulsing until finely chopped, then add the yogurt and lime juice and process until smooth. Cover and refrigerate until serving time.

2. Prepare grill for direct heat and preheat to medium-high.

3. Brush the salmon fillets with olive oil on both sides. Season with salt and pepper.

4. Oil the grill grates. Place the salmon skin-side down directly over the heat and grill without moving for 4 minutes or until the salmon releases without sticking. Flip and cook for another 2 minutes or until the flesh is opaque. Serve with the sauce.

SERVES 4

Duke visits the Parthenon in Athens in 1956.

AMERICAN GRILL FACTS

Of the seven species of Pacific salmon, Chinook (or king) salmon are the largest and most rich-tasting, due to their high fat content.

UPSCALE TUNA SALAD NIÇOISE

Serve your loved ones a taste of the French Riviera without leaving the comforts of your backyard. This Mediterranean classic comes together in minutes.

PROVISIONS

- ¼ cup red wine vinegar
- 1 small shallot, finely minced
- 1 tsp. Dijon mustard
- 1 garlic clove, finely grated
- ½ cup olive oil plus more for the tuna and bread
- 1½ lb. small (1–2 inches) red potatoes, cut in half
- Kosher or fine sea salt
- ¾ lb. French green beans, trimmed
- 1 pint cherry or grape tomatoes
- 1½ lb. fresh tuna steaks
- Black pepper
- 2 baguettes
- Vegetable oil for the grill
- 1 large head Boston lettuce
- 6 large hard boiled eggs, peeled and cut in half lengthwise
- ⅔ cup pitted kalamata niçoise olives

PREP

1. Combine vinegar, shallot, mustard, garlic and ½ cup olive oil in a jar with a pinch of salt and pepper. Shake the jar well to emulsify.

2. Place potatoes in a large pot and cover with cold water. Add 2 tsp. salt and bring to a boil. Let cook for 10 to 15 minutes or until fork tender. Drain, put the potatoes back in the pan with 2 Tbsp. of the dressing, toss to coat and let cool.

3. Bring a pot of lightly salted water to a boil and prepare a bowl of ice water. Add the green beans to the pot and cook for 2 minutes or until crisp tender, then immediately submerge in the ice water. Drain off the water, add 2 tsp. of the dressing and toss to coat.

4. Put the tomatoes in a small bowl with 2 tsp. of the dressing and toss to coat. Brush the tuna steaks with olive oil, season on both sides with salt and pepper and let sit at room temperature while the grill heats. Cut the baguettes in half, brush with olive oil and season with salt and pepper.

5. Prepare grill for direct heat and preheat to medium-high. Oil the grates with vegetable oil.

6. Grill the bread over direct heat with the lid closed for 4 to 5 minutes or until charred and warm. Remove from grill and keep warm. Slice before serving.

7. Place the tuna steaks directly over the flames and grill for 2 minutes per side. Let rest until cool enough to handle then slice thinly.

8. Arrange the lettuce on a large platter and lightly drizzle with dressing. Top with the potatoes, green beans, tomatoes, eggs, tuna and olives on the platter. Serve with sliced bread.

SERVES 6

WAYNE FAMILY TIP

For added authentic flair, throw some anchovies on the grill to serve with your salad. Grill covered on medium heat for 3 to 4 minutes, flip, cover and grill for another 3 to 4 minutes before serving.

GRILLED TILAPIA AND PESTO VEGETABLES

Even the pickiest eaters won't be able to resist the tempting aromas of this grilled fish.

PROVISIONS

- 1 zucchini, diced
- 1 yellow summer squash, diced
- 1 red bell pepper, seeded, deveined and diced
- 1 pint cherry or grape tomatoes
- 1 small shallot, minced
- ½ cup prepared green pesto
- Heavy duty aluminum foil
- 4 (6-oz.) tilapia fillets
- Kosher or fine sea salt
- Black pepper
- 2 lemons

PREP

1. Prepare grill for direct heat and preheat to medium.

2. Combine the vegetables in a large mixing bowl with the pesto. Stir to coat all the vegetables well.

3. Tear four sheets of foil about 24 inches long and place on a flat work surface. Divide the vegetables evenly among the foil pieces, then place in the center of each foil piece in a flat layer. Sprinkle both sides of the tilapia fillets with salt and pepper and place on top of the vegetables. Seal the foil securely and grill, covered, for 10 minutes.

4. During the last 5 minutes of grilling, cut the lemons in half and grill until charred and soft.

5. Serve in the foil packets.

SERVES 4

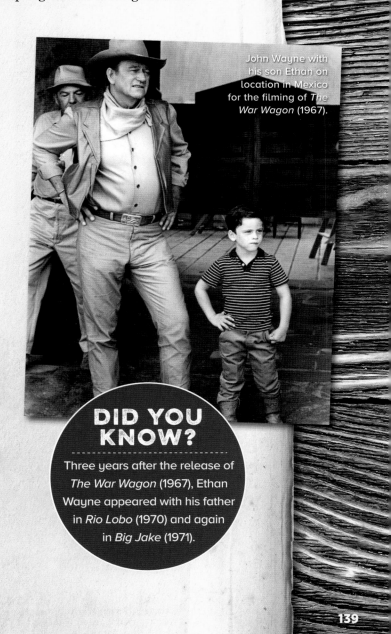

John Wayne with his son Ethan on location in Mexico for the filming of *The War Wagon* (1967).

DID YOU KNOW?

Three years after the release of *The War Wagon* (1967), Ethan Wayne appeared with his father in *Rio Lobo* (1970) and again in *Big Jake* (1971).

RED WITCH TILAPIA TACOS
WITH CHERRY CHIPOTLE SALSA

Sweet, spicy and effortlessly customizable, these tacos will have your guests spellbound.

PROVISIONS

- 2 **cups thawed frozen sweet cherries, cut into quarters**
- 1 **clove garlic, minced**
- ¼ **cup red onion, roughly chopped**
- 1 **chipotle pepper in adobo sauce (or 1-2 tsp. pureed chipotle in adobo)**
- ¼ **cup cilantro leaves**
- **Juice of 1 lime**
- 1½ **tsp. ground cumin**
- ¾ **tsp. salt**
- ¼ **tsp. black pepper**
- 6 **(4–6 oz. each) tilapia fillets**
- 2 **Tbsp. olive oil**
- **Vegetable oil for the grill basket or grill**
- 12 **corn tortillas**
- 2 **cups finely shredded cabbage**
- **Lime wedges and cilantro, for serving**

PREP

1. Dry the cherries on paper towels. Place the garlic and red onion in a food processor and pulse to chop. Add the chipotle in adobo, cilantro leaves and lime juice and pulse to combine. Add the cherries and pulse just until they are roughly chopped. Place in a small serving dish and reserve.

2. Prepare grill for direct heat and preheat to medium.

3. Combine the ground cumin, salt and pepper in a small bowl. Brush the tilapia fillets on both sides with olive oil and sprinkle with cumin seasoning.

4. If using a grill basket, oil generously. If cooking directly on the grill, oil the grates. Grill for 2 minutes, then flip and grill on the other side for 2 or 3 more minutes or until the fish is cooked through and starts to flake. When done, flake the fish into a serving bowl and cover to keep warm.

5. Place the tortillas directly on the grill and grill for about 45 seconds or until charred and warm. Serve with the fish, cabbage, salsa, lime wedges and cilantro.

SERVES 6 (2 TACOS PER PERSON)

John Wayne in *Wake of the Red Witch* (1948).

BLACKENED GROUPER SANDWICHES

A mainstay of the Gulf of Mexico, the Florida Keys and the Caribbean, grouper is a delightfully mild-tasting fish that makes for firm, flaky, mouthwatering sandwiches no matter the season. These grilled sliders are no exception.

PROVISIONS

½	cup mayonnaise
⅓	cup finely chopped dill pickles
3	Tbsp. very finely minced white onion
2	Tbsp. fresh parsley, minced then measured
2	tsp. lemon juice
1	tsp. sugar
¼	tsp. black pepper
⅛	tsp. garlic powder
⅛	tsp. onion powder
4	(6-oz.) grouper fillets 1½-inches thick (can also use sea bass, snapper or mahi mahi)
	Olive oil
	Cajun seasoning
	Vegetable oil for the grill
4	hamburger buns
4	thick slices tomato
4	lettuce leaves

Duke and actor William Bendix enjoy the open seas aboard an ocean liner in 1954.

AMERICAN GRILL FACTS

Florida harvests more than 85 percent of all the grouper available in the U.S., most of which first comes ashore in Pinellas County.

PREP

TARTAR SAUCE

1. Combine the mayonnaise, pickles, onion, parsley, lemon juice, sugar, pepper and garlic and onion powders in a small bowl and mix well. Cover and refrigerate until serving time.

FISH

1. Prepare grill for direct heat and preheat to medium.

2. Brush the fish fillets on all sides with olive oil. Season on all sides with Cajun seasoning.

3. Oil the grill grates well. Grill the fish fillets over direct flame with the lid closed for 4 minutes per side. Remove from the grill, brush the cut sides of the burger buns with olive oil and grill for about 1 minute or until lightly toasted.

4. Serve with lettuce, tomato and tartar sauce.

SERVES 4

MEXICAN-STYLE WHOLE FISH STUFFED
WITH CILANTRO AND LIME

When he wasn't on a film set or sailing on the *Wild Goose*, Duke enjoyed traveling to Mexico, especially the coastal city of Acapulco, where simple but filling dishes like this grilled whole fish make for an unforgettable meal.

PROVISIONS

1 (approximately 3-lb.) whole fish such as red snapper, sea bass or branzino, cleaned and scaled

   Olive oil

   Kosher or fine sea salt

   Black pepper

1 small bunch fresh cilantro

1 lime, sliced

1 serrano chile, cut in half lengthwise

3 large red onions

   Vegetable oil for the grill

   Lime wedges, for serving

PREP

1. Prepare grill for direct heat and preheat to medium-high.

2. Using kitchen shears, cut the fins off the fish, then rinse and dry the fish, inside and out. Using a sharp knife, cut three to four deep slits into the flesh of the fish. Brush well with olive oil and season generously with salt and pepper, inside and out.

3. Fill the cavity of the fish with the cilantro, lime slices and chile. Peel the onions and cut into ½-inch thick slices. Brush both sides of the onion slices with olive oil.

4. Oil the grill grates well. Lay the onion slices down on the grill to create a bed for the fish. Place the fish on top of the onion slices and grill with the lid closed for 8 minutes. Flip the fish and grill for another 8 minutes. Remove the fish from the onions, then remove the onions from the grill and set aside. Place the fish back on the grill for 1 minute per side to crisp the skin.

5. Remove the cilantro lime filling from the cavity of the fish and serve with the grilled onions and lime wedges.

SERVES 4

Fall-Off-the-Bone
Baby Back Ribs, p. 164

PORK

Versatile, delicious and easy on the wallet, give pork the proper attention and watch it become the star of your grilling repertoire.

J.B. Books's Barbecue Pork Tenderloins

Italian Sausage and Pepper Sandwiches

Brannigan's Cider Brats with Apples and Onions

Pork Paillard with Zucchini and Romesco Sauce

Sofrito Pork Chops

Cherry Chipotle BBQ Pork Tenderloins

Citrus-Brined Pork Loin with Orange Mustard

Fall-Off-the-Bone Baby Back Ribs

Red River Ribs

Knockout Maple-Brined Pork Chops

Cider-Brined Pork Chops with Grilled Apples

Fancy Herb-Stuffed Pork Loin

Mojo Pork Tenderloin with Grilled Onions

Tapenade-Stuffed Bacon-Wrapped Pork Loin

Donovan's Reef Jerk Pork with Pineapple Salsa and Plantains

Blue Ribbon Smoked Boston Butt

J.B. BOOKS'S BARBECUE PORK TENDERLOINS

Famished guests won't dare think of insulting your cooking once they lay their hands on these satisfying tenderloins.

PROVISIONS

- ½ cup barbecue sauce
- ½ cup orange marmalade
- ¼ cup ketchup
- 2 Tbsp. Sriracha sauce
- 2 Tbsp. Worcestershire sauce
- 1 tsp. garlic powder
- 2 (1–1¼ lb. each) pork tenderloins

PREP

1. Combine the barbecue sauce, marmalade, ketchup, Sriracha, Worcestershire sauce and garlic powder in a medium mixing bowl and mix well. Pour half of the sauce into a large food storage bag, add the pork tenderloins, squeeze out excess air and refrigerate for 1 to 12 hours. Place the rest of the sauce in a small bowl, cover and refrigerate until ready to grill the pork.

2. Remove the pork from the refrigerator, discard the marinade and let sit at room temperature for 15 to 20 minutes.

3. Prepare grill for direct heat and preheat to medium-high. Grill the pork for 10 to 12 minutes or until it reaches an internal temperature of 140 degrees F, turning every 2 minutes.

4. Place the tenderloins on a piece of aluminum foil, brush with half the remaining sauce, wrap and let sit for 5 minutes before slicing. Serve the rest of the sauce on the side.

SERVES 6

John Wayne in *The Shootist* (1976).

DID YOU KNOW?

John Wayne recorded a public service announcement for the American Cancer Society that began with a clip from *The Shootist* (1976).

ITALIAN SAUSAGE AND PEPPER SANDWICHES

Whether you choose sweet or spicy sausages for these savory bites is up to you. We say bring on the heat.

PROVISIONS

- 2 Tbsp. olive oil
- 1 medium white or yellow onion, thinly sliced
- 1 red bell pepper, seeded, deveined and thinly sliced
- 1 green bell pepper, seeded, deveined and thinly sliced
- 1 tsp. kosher or fine sea salt
- ½ tsp. pepper
- 6 Italian sausages
- 6 hoagie rolls

PREP

1. Heat oil in a large skillet over medium-high heat. Add the onion and cook, stirring occasionally, until soft, about 5 minutes. Add the peppers, salt and pepper, then cook, stirring occasionally, until the peppers are soft and the vegetables are starting to brown, about 10 minutes. Keep warm.

2. Prepare the grill for direct heat and preheat to medium-high.

3. Prick the sausages with a fork in several places to keep them from bursting. Grill with the lid closed for 10 to 12 minutes, turning every 2 minutes or until browned on the outside and juices run clear.

4. Serve the sausages on hoagie rolls topped with onions and peppers.

SERVES 6

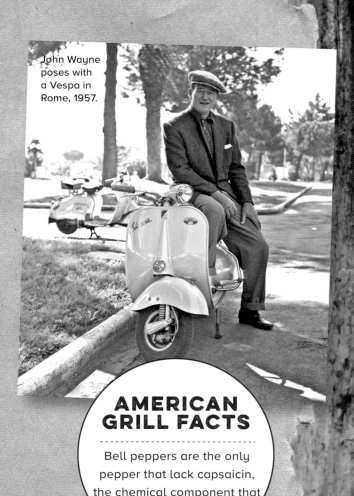

John Wayne poses with a Vespa in Rome, 1957.

AMERICAN GRILL FACTS

Bell peppers are the only pepper that lack capsaicin, the chemical component that gives chiles their heat.

BRANNIGAN'S CIDER BRATS
WITH APPLES AND ONIONS

Break out this Midwestern cookout classic for an instant Oktoberfest-style feast that works any time of year.

PROVISIONS

- ¾   cup mayonnaise
- 6   Tbsp. ketchup
- 2   Tbsp. chopped pickled jalapeños
- 1   tsp. Dijon mustard
-      Vegetable oil
- 6   bratwurst
- 1   disposable aluminum roasting pan
- 3   (12-oz.) bottles hard apple cider
- 8   Tbsp. unsalted butter
- 1   large white onion, sliced
- 2   apples, cored and sliced
- 1   cup sauerkraut, drained
- 6   hoagie rolls

John Wayne in
Brannigan (1975).

PREP

1. Combine the mayonnaise, ketchup, jalapeños and mustard and stir until combined. Cover and refrigerate until serving time.

2. Prepare grill for direct and indirect heat and preheat to medium-high. Oil the grates on both sides. Brush the bratwurst with oil. Place the cider, butter, onion and apples in the aluminum pan over direct heat.

3. Char the brats over direct heat for about 5 minutes, turning often. Move to the indirect side of the grill and cook with the lid closed for 10 minutes per side or until the brats reach an internal temperature of 150–155 degrees F. Place the brats in the cider bath and cook with the lid closed for another 10 to 15 minutes or until the onions and apples are softened and starting to brown and the brats reach an internal temperature of 160 degrees F.

4. Put the sauerkraut in a grill-proof skillet and heat over direct heat just until warmed. Oil the hoagie rolls and lightly toast.

5. To serve, spread some of the sauce on the rolls and add sauerkraut, brats, apples, onions and more sauce if desired.

SERVES 6

PORK PAILLARD
WITH ZUCCHINI AND ROMESCO SAUCE

For a taste of Barcelona you can cook right in your backyard, this rustic pork dish features romesco sauce, a Catalonian tomato-based condiment that's sure to delight the senses.

PROVISIONS

- 1 (12-oz.) jar roasted red peppers, drained
- ½ cup sliced almonds
- Olive oil
- 1 Tbsp. fresh lemon juice
- 1 clove garlic, minced
- 1 tsp. hot paprika
- Kosher or fine sea salt
- Black pepper
- 4 boneless center-cut pork chops, 6–7 oz. each and about 1 inch thick
- 3 zucchini
- Vegetable oil

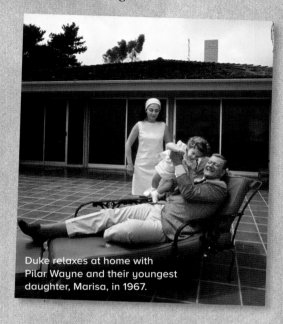

Duke relaxes at home with Pilar Wayne and their youngest daughter, Marisa, in 1967.

PREP

1. Combine peppers, almonds, 1 Tbsp. olive oil, lemon juice, garlic and hot paprika in a food processor and pulse until semi-smooth. Season to taste with salt and pepper.

2. Prepare the grill for direct heat and preheat to medium-high. Oil the grates.

3. Starting with the fat side, cut the chops in half horizontally and trim the excess fat. Flatten out the meat like a book and, one at a time, place the chops between two sheets of waxed paper and pound with a meat mallet or rolling pin until each piece has an even thickness of about ¼ inch. Brush both sides with olive oil and season with salt and pepper.

4. Cut both ends of the zucchini off and slice vertically about ¼ inch thick. Brush with olive oil and season with salt and pepper.

5. Grill the pork and zucchini over direct heat with the lid closed for 3 minutes. Flip the pork and continue cooking for 1 to 2 minutes or until the meat is slightly pink when pierced with the tip of a sharp knife. Grill the zucchini for 2 to 3 more minutes or until softened.

6. Serve the pork on top of the zucchini slices topped with the sauce.

SERVES 4

John Wayne and
Marguerite Churchill in
The Big Trail (1930).
Churchill also appeared
with Duke in *Born Reckless*
(1930) and *Girls Demand
Excitement* (1931).

SOFRITO PORK CHOPS

Commonly found in Spanish-speaking countries across Latin America and Europe, sofrito is an aromatic comfort food sauce that will take your grilling scene by storm.

PROVISIONS

- 4 bone-in rib pork chops ¾–1 inch thick
- Vegetable oil
- 1 tsp. kosher or fine sea salt
- ½ tsp. black pepper
- ½ tsp. dried cumin
- 1 (12-oz.) jar sofrito tomato base sauce

PREP

1. Rinse pork chops and dry well. Brush both sides with oil. Combine the salt, pepper and cumin in a small bowl. Sprinkle the mixture on both sides of the chops. Let the chops sit at room temperature while the grill heats.

2. Prepare grill for direct heat. Place a large cast-iron skillet on the grill and preheat grill to medium-high.

3. When the grill is hot, pour the sofrito sauce into the skillet and nestle the pork chops in the sauce. Cook, covered, for 7 minutes with the lid closed. Turn the chops over and cook for another 6 to 8 minutes or until the chops reach an internal temperature of 145 degrees F.

4. Top the chops with the sauce before serving.

SERVES 4

Duke and Pilar Wayne play gin rummy in an undated photo.

DID YOU KNOW?

Duke met his wife, Pilar Pallete, in her native country of Peru while scouting locations to film his passion project, *The Alamo* (1960).

CHERRY CHIPOTLE BBQ PORK TENDERLOINS

Cola's the key ingredient in elevating this sauce from ordinary to otherworldly. Making the most of your seasonal summer fruit never tasted so good.

PROVISIONS

- ½ **cup barbecue sauce**
- ½ **cup cherry jelly**
- ¼ **cup ketchup**
- 2 **Tbsp. Sriracha sauce**
- 2 **Tbsp. pureed chipotles in adobo sauce**
- 1 **tsp. garlic powder**
- 1 **cup cola (not diet)**
- 2 **(1–1¼ lb. each) pork tenderloins**

PREP

1. Combine the barbecue sauce, jelly, ketchup, Sriracha, chipotles and garlic powder in a medium mixing bowl and mix well. Pour half of the sauce into a bowl and add the cola. Pour the cola mixture into a large food storage bag, add the pork tenderloins, squeeze out any excess air and refrigerate for 1 hour or up to 12 hours.

2. Meanwhile, place the rest of the sauce in a small bowl, cover and refrigerate until ready to grill the pork. Remove the pork from the refrigerator, discard the marinade and let sit at room temperature for 15 to 20 minutes.

3. Prepare grill for direct heat and preheat to medium-high. Grill the pork for 10 to 12 minutes or until it reaches an internal temperature of 140 degrees F, turning every 2 minutes.

4. Place the tenderloins on a piece of aluminum foil, brush with half the remaining sauce, wrap and let sit for 5 minutes before slicing. Serve the rest of the sauce on the side.

SERVES 6

John Wayne spends quality time with a four-legged friend, c. 1950s.

CITRUS-BRINED PORK LOIN
WITH ORANGE MUSTARD

This pork loin dish is a labor of love that's sure to win top marks at the dinner table. Infusing your meat with citrus and letting it marinate overnight adds a little zing and helps ensure it won't dry out on the grill.

PROVISIONS

- 1 (1½-lb.) pork tenderloin
- Vegetable oil
- Pepper

BRINE

- 3 cups warm water
- ½ cup kosher salt
- ½ cup sugar
- ½ cup fresh orange juice (from 2 large oranges)
- 2 bay leaves
- 3 cups ice

ORANGE MUSTARD

- ½ cup orange marmalade
- 1½ Tbsp. Dijon mustard
- 1 tsp. honey
- ½ tsp. garlic powder

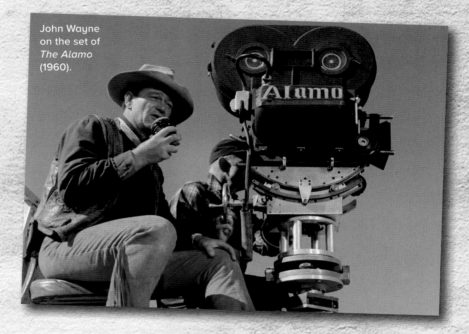

John Wayne on the set of *The Alamo* (1960).

PREP

1. To make the brine, combine the warm water with the salt, sugar, orange juice and bay leaves, stirring until sugar and salt have dissolved. Add the ice and stir until the mixture is cool.

2. Pour the brine mixture into a large food storage bag. Add the pork tenderloin, squeeze out the air from the bag and seal. Place in the refrigerator for 2 to 12 hours. Remove from the refrigerator, discard the brine, rinse the pork with cold water and let sit at room temperature for 15 to 20 minutes. Brush with oil and season with pepper.

3. Prepare grill for direct heat and preheat to medium-high. Grill the pork for 10 to 12 minutes or until it reaches an internal temperature of 140 degrees F, turning every 2 minutes. Cover with foil and let sit for 5 minutes before slicing.

4. To make the orange mustard, combine all ingredients and mix well. Serve with the pork.

SERVES 4

FALL-OFF-THE-BONE BABY BACK RIBS

The ideal meal for any lazy afternoon, this finger-licking barbecue favorite is perfection on a plate.

PROVISIONS

DRY RUB

- ¼ medium white or yellow onion
- 2 Tbsp. olive oil
- 2 tsp. kosher or fine sea salt
- 2 cloves garlic, minced
- 1 Tbsp. chili powder
- 1 tsp. black pepper
- 1 tsp. ground cumin
- 1 tsp. allspice

RIBS

- 2 racks of pork baby back ribs
- Dry rub (above) or your favorite dry rub
- Barbecue sauce (below) or your favorite barbecue sauce

BARBECUE SAUCE

- 1 cup ketchup
- ½ cup molasses
- ½ cup honey
- ¾ cup pineapple juice
- 1 Tbsp. Worcestershire sauce
- 1 Tbsp. garlic powder
- 1 Tbsp. onion powder
- ½ tsp. kosher or fine sea salt
- ½ tsp. black pepper
- 6 dashes hot sauce (such as Tabasco)
- 1 Tbsp. pureed chipotle in adobo sauce

PREP

1. Combine all the dry rub ingredients in a small bowl, mixing well. (Can be stored in an airtight container for up to 6 months.)

2. Flip the ribs bone side up on a cutting board or other flat clean surface and insert a dinner knife just beneath the white membrane that covers the meat and bones. Gently peel off the membrane.

3. Place ribs in a rimmed baking sheet or large foil roasting pan. Season generously on both sides with the dry rub. Refrigerate uncovered for 30 minutes or up to 4 hours.

4. Meanwhile, combine all the barbecue sauce ingredients in a large saucepan and whisk well. Bring to a boil over high heat. Once it begins to boil, reduce heat and simmer, stirring occasionally, for 30 minutes or until the sauce is thick and glossy. Whisk the sauce well. (Can be stored, covered, in the refrigerator for up to a month.)

5. Prepare grill for direct and indirect heat. Place heavy duty foil or a disposable aluminum pan under the grates of the indirect side of the grill and preheat to medium-low (around 250 degrees F). Oil the grates. Place the ribs on the indirect side of the grill, close the lid and cook for 2½ to 3 hours.

6. You can tell the ribs are done when they have shrunk away from most of the bones by ¼ inch or more or when a rack is lifted with tongs at one end and it bends in the middle and the meat tears away easily. When the ribs are fully cooked, brush with barbecue sauce, move to the direct side of the grill and grill on both sides until the sauce starts to caramelize, 2 to 3 minutes. Serve with extra sauce on the side.

SERVES 6–8

RED RIVER RIBS

Whether you're feeding a hardy team of cowhands or catering your neighborhood block party, these mouthwatering ribs don't disappoint.

PROVISIONS

- 2 racks of pork baby back ribs
- 3 cups wood chips, soaked in water for a least 1 hour

BARBECUE SAUCE

- 2 Tbsp. olive oil
- 1 small white onion, very finely diced
- 2 cups ketchup
- ½ cup molasses
- ½ cup brown sugar, packed
- ½ cup apple juice
- ½ cup apple cider vinegar
- 2 Tbsp. paprika
- 1 Tbsp. garlic powder
- 1 tsp. kosher or fine sea salt
- 1 tsp. black pepper
  Hot sauce, to taste

DRY RUB

- 2 Tbsp. kosher or fine sea salt
- 1 Tbsp. brown sugar
- 1 Tbsp. ground cumin
- 1 Tbsp. paprika
- 1 Tbsp. garlic powder
- 1 Tbsp. onion powder
- 1 Tbsp. chili powder
- 1 tsp. cayenne pepper
- 1 tsp. black pepper

MOP SAUCE

- ½ Tbsp. kosher or fine sea salt
- ½ Tbsp. brown sugar
- 3 Tbsp. ground cumin
- 2 Tbsp. dry rub (left)

PREP

1. To make the barbecue sauce, heat olive oil in a medium saucepan over medium-high heat. Add the onions and cook, stirring occasionally, until tender, about 5 minutes. Add the ketchup, molasses, brown sugar, apple juice, vinegar, paprika, garlic powder, salt and pepper. Bring mixture to a gentle boil, reduce heat and simmer uncovered for 30 to 40 minutes. Add hot sauce to taste. Remove from heat and let cool. (Can be made ahead 1 week and stored, covered, in the refrigerator.)

2. Whisk all the dry rub ingredients together in a small bowl. (Can be stored for 6 months in an airtight container.)

3. Whisk all the mop sauce ingredients together in a small bowl until thoroughly combined. Let sit to allow the flavors to mingle. (Can be made ahead and stored for up to 1 week, covered, in the refrigerator.)

4. Flip the ribs bone side up on a cutting board or other flat clean surface and insert a dinner knife just under the white membrane that covers the meat and bones. Gently peel off the membrane. Place ribs on a rimmed baking sheet or large foil roasting pan. Season generously on both sides with the dry rub. Refrigerate uncovered for 30 minutes or up to 4 hours.

5. Prepare grill for indirect heat. If using a charcoal grill, rake the lit coals into two piles on opposite sides of the grill and place a drip pan in the center. Place wood chips directly on the coals. Heat grill to medium-low, 250 degrees F. If using a gas grill, place wood chips in a smoker box and place under a grate directly over an unlit burner or two, preferably a back corner. Place a drip pan on the indirect side of the grill. Turn the other burners on high and heat until smoke starts. Lower the temperature to medium-low, 250 degrees F.

6. Place the ribs, bone-side down, directly on the grill over indirect heat. Cover the grill, maintaining a temperature of about 250 degrees F. After 30 minutes, gently mop with the mop sauce. Continue grilling the ribs, mopping every 20 to 30 minutes, until the ribs are done, 3 to 4 hours. Start checking the meat at 3 hours. You can tell the ribs are done when they have shrunk away from most of the bones by ¼ inch or more and when a rack is lifted with tongs at one end and it bends in the middle and the meat tears away easily. When this occurs, baste with barbecue sauce and cook for another 10 minutes. You can place the ribs on oiled racks over the direct heat for 1 to 2 minutes to caramelize the sauce if desired. Serve with extra barbecue sauce.

SERVES 4–6

John Wayne and Joanne Dru in *Red River* (1948).

KNOCKOUT MAPLE-BRINED PORK CHOPS

Punch up your outdoor table spread with this show-stopping dish that tastes as heavenly as it smells.

PROVISIONS

- ½ cup plus 2 Tbsp. maple syrup, divided
- ½ cup kosher salt
- 3 Tbsp. plus 1 tsp. Dijon mustard, divided
- 2 Tbsp. fresh rosemary, minced
- Black pepper
- 2 cups water
- 4 cups ice
- 4 center-cut loin pork chops (approximately 1 inch thick)
- Vegetable oil

PREP

1. Combine ½ cup maple syrup, salt, 3 Tbsp. Dijon mustard, rosemary and 1 tsp. pepper with the water in a saucepan and bring to a boil, stirring to dissolve the salt. Take off the heat, then stir in the ice. Pour the brining liquid into a large plastic food storage bag, add the chops, squeeze out any excess air, seal the bag and refrigerate for 1 to 12 hours.

2. Remove from refrigerator, discard the brine, rinse the pork with cold water and let sit at room temperature for 15 to 20 minutes. Brush with oil and season with pepper.

3. Prepare grill for direct heat and indirect heat and preheat to medium-high. Combine the remaining 2 Tbsp. maple syrup with the remaining 1 tsp. of Dijon mustard.

4. Grill the chops for 3 minutes over direct heat, flip and grill for another 3 minutes. Move the chops to the indirect heat side of the grill, close the lid and grill for another 7 to 8 minutes, turning once, or until they reach an internal temperature of 140 degrees F. Brush the chops with the maple/mustard sauce and let sit for 5 minutes before serving.

SERVES 4

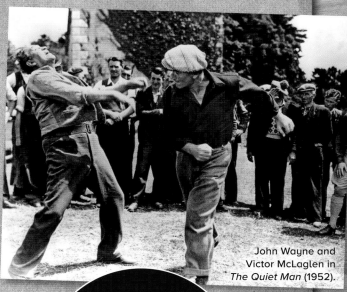

John Wayne and Victor McLaglen in *The Quiet Man* (1952).

DID YOU KNOW?

John Ford's love letter to Ireland, *The Quiet Man* (1952) won two Academy Awards for Best Cinematography, Color and Best Director.

John Wayne in *The Cowboys* (1972). The film spawned a one-season television series that ran in 1974 and featured four of the original cast members.

CIDER-BRINED PORK CHOPS
WITH GRILLED APPLES

When there's a chill in the air, between the hard cider and the apple slices sizzling on the grill, this hearty meal hits the spot like no other.

PROVISIONS

- 2 (12-oz.) bottles hard apple cider
- ½ cup kosher salt
- 4 sprigs fresh rosemary
- 2 sprigs fresh thyme
- 1 tsp. whole black peppercorns
- 4 boneless center cut pork chops, about 1 inch thick
  Olive oil
  Black pepper
  Vegetable oil
- 3 Granny Smith apples, sliced into ½-inch circles
- 2 Tbsp. melted butter
- 3 Tbsp. brown sugar
- 1 tsp. ground cinnamon

PREP

1. Combine the cider, salt, herbs and peppercorns in a large bowl and stir to dissolve the salt. Place the pork chops in a large resealable food storage bag and pour in the brine. Squeeze out any excess air, seal the bag and refrigerate for 1½ to 4 hours, turning the bag over every 30 minutes.

2. Remove the chops from the brine, rinse with cold water, pat dry, brush with olive oil on both sides and sprinkle with a pinch of ground pepper. Let sit at room temperature while the grill heats and you prepare the apples.

3. Brush a grill basket with vegetable oil. Brush the apple slices on both sides with melted butter. Combine the brown sugar and cinnamon in a small bowl. Sprinkle the mixture on both sides of the apple slices before placing them in the grill basket.

4. Prepare grill for direct heat and preheat to medium-high. Oil the grates with vegetable oil.

5. Grill the pork for 4 minutes per side with the lid closed or until it reaches an internal temperature of 145 degrees F. Grill the apples for 6 minutes per side with the lid closed. Let the pork chops rest while the apples finish cooking.

SERVES 4

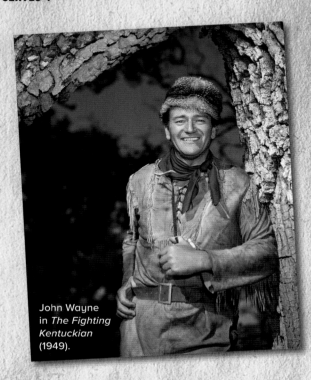

John Wayne in *The Fighting Kentuckian* (1949).

FANCY HERB-STUFFED PORK LOIN

For a stress-free day of outdoor cooking, you can prep this tasty rolled loin a day ahead, then throw it on the grill when you're good and ready.

PROVISIONS

- ¼ **cup fresh sage leaves, plus sprigs for serving**
- ¼ **cup fresh thyme leaves, plus sprigs for serving**
- 2 **Tbsp. fresh rosemary leaves, plus more for serving**
- 3 **cloves garlic**
- 5 **Tbsp. olive oil**
- 1 **tsp. Dijon mustard**
- 1 **tsp. kosher or fine sea salt**
- ½ **tsp. black pepper**
- ¼ **tsp. crushed red pepper flakes**
- 1 **(3-lb.) pork loin roast**

PREP

1. Combine the herbs, garlic, olive oil, mustard, salt, pepper and pepper flakes in a small food processor and pulse until it forms a loose paste.

2. Place the pork loin fat-side down on a cutting board. Using a long, sharp knife, make a horizontal slice lengthwise about ⅓ of the way from the bottom stopping about one inch from the other side. Open the flap. Make another horizontal cut halfway into thicker side of the roast, starting from the centfacrser and working toward the outer edge. Open the flap, creating a flat piece of meat. Gently pound with a mallet or rolling pin until even.

3. Rub ⅔ of the paste on the inside of the roast. Roll the roast up tightly and tie with kitchen string at 1½- to 2-inch intervals. Rub the rest of the paste on the outside of the roast. Let roast sit at room temperature while the grill heats or store in the refrigerator for up to 24 hours.

4. Prepare grill for direct and indirect heat and preheat to medium. Oil the grates.

5. Place the roast over direct heat and sear on four sides for 2 to 3 minutes per side. Transfer to the indirect side, close the lid and cook, turning a quarter turn every 15 minutes, until the roast reaches an internal temperature of 145 degrees F, about 1 hour and 15 minutes. Remove roast from grill, cover loosely with foil and let rest for 15 minutes before removing the string and slicing.

SERVES 6

Duke attends the Academy Awards on March 25, 1954.

WAYNE FAMILY TIP

For authentic Cuban flair, swap out the cilantro for oregano. You can also use the mojo as a dipping sauce for plantain chips or fried yuca.

MOJO PORK TENDERLOIN
WITH GRILLED ONIONS

Bursting with bold citrus flavor, this Cuban dish will take your taste buds to places that evoke breezy nights on moonlit beaches.

PROVISIONS

- 1 **cup fresh orange juice (from 2–3 large oranges)**
- 1 **cup fresh lime juice (from 6–8 large limes)**
- 4 **garlic cloves, minced**
- 1 **Tbsp. ground cumin**
- **Kosher or fine sea salt**
- **Black pepper**
- ½ **cup olive oil, plus more for brushing the onions**
- ¼ **cup chopped fresh cilantro, plus more for garnish**
- 1 **(1½-lb.) pork tenderloin**
- 1 **orange, sliced**
- 2 **large white onions**
- **Vegetable oil**

PREP

1. Combine the orange and lime juices, garlic, cumin, 1½ tsp. salt and 1 tsp. pepper in a bowl and whisk to combine. Remove ½ cup and save covered in the refrigerator.

2. Add the olive oil and cilantro to the bowl with the citrus mixture, stir and pour into a large resealable food storage bag. Add the pork and the sliced orange and let marinate for 6 to 24 hours. Remove the pork and orange slices from the marinade and discard the marinade. Let the pork sit at room temperature.

3. Meanwhile, prepare the grill for direct heat and preheat to medium. Oil the grates with vegetable oil. Thickly slice the onions and brush both sides with olive oil. Season both sides with salt and pepper and place in an oiled grill basket.

4. Grill the pork over direct heat with the lid closed and flip every 5 to 6 minutes for 20 to 30 minutes or until it reaches an internal temperature of 145 degrees F. Remove from the grill and let rest while you grill the onions and orange slices.

5. Place the grill basket with the onions and orange slices on the grill and grill with the lid closed for 2 to 3 minutes per side or until charred and the onions are soft. Place the reserved marinade in a saucepan and cook over direct heat until it has reduced by half, about 5 minutes.

6. Slice the pork, serve over the onions and orange slices and drizzle with the mojo sauce. Garnish with cilantro if desired.

SERVES 4–6

Duke and his sons Michael and Patrick on the set of *Hondo* (1953).

TAPENADE-STUFFED BACON-WRAPPED PORK LOIN

It's a simple law of the universe that anything wrapped in bacon, the king of crispy meats, is bound to taste incredible. Set this pork loin on the table and watch your guests come running.

PROVISIONS

1	(3-lb.) pork loin roast
	Tapenade (recipe below)
5–6	slices bacon, not thick cut
	Vegetable oil

TAPENADE

12	oz. pitted Kalamata olives, drained
2	oil-packed anchovy fillets, minced
3	Tbsp. capers in brine, rinsed
3	garlic cloves, chopped
3	Tbsp. fresh lemon juice
¼	tsp. red pepper flakes
¼	cup olive oil
	Kosher or fine sea salt
	Black pepper

PREP

1. Combine olives, anchovies, capers, garlic, lemon juice and red pepper flakes in a small food processor and pulse until coarsely chopped. With the machine running, slowly add the olive oil and process until the mixture forms a paste, scraping down the sides of the bowl as needed. Taste and add salt and pepper if desired. Store at room temperature.

2. Place the pork loin fat-side down on a cutting board. Using a long, sharp knife, make a horizontal slice lengthwise about ⅓ of the way from the bottom stopping about one inch from the other side. Open the flap. Make another horizontal cut halfway into thicker side of the roast, starting from the center and working toward the outer edge. Open the flap, creating a flat piece of meat. Gently pound with a mallet or rolling pin until even. Spread the tapenade over the cut surface.

3. Roll the pork up tightly, back into its original shape. Wrap bacon slices around the outside of the roast, covering the outside. Using kitchen string, tie up the roast in 1- to 2-inch intervals. Let the roast sit at room temperature while the grill heats.

4. Prepare the grill for direct and indirect heat and preheat to medium. Oil the grates.

5. Place the roast on the indirect side of the grill and cook with the lid closed for 45 to 60 minutes or until it reaches an internal temperature of 140 degrees F, turning the roast every 6 minutes. Start checking the temperature at the 40-minute mark. If the bacon is not crispy enough when the pork has come to temperature, put over direct heat for a few minutes per side. Let the roast rest for 10 minutes before slicing.

SERVES 6

Duke and Pilar Wayne at home with their children Ethan, Aissa and Marisa, c. 1969.

WAYNE FAMILY TIP

If you have leftover tapenade, save it and serve on toasted baguette slices for crowd-pleasing small bites.

DONOVAN'S REEF JERK PORK
WITH PINEAPPLE SALSA AND PLANTAINS

You might want to cook this recipe in ample batches, pilgrim, lest your guests throw down over who gets seconds.

PROVISIONS

- 1 bunch green onions, chopped
- ½ small white onion, chopped
- 2 cloves garlic, chopped
- 1–4 Scotch bonnet or habanero peppers (depending on desired heat level), seeded and chopped
- 2 Tbsp. white vinegar
- 1 Tbsp. soy sauce
- Vegetable oil
- 1 Tbsp. brown sugar
- 2 tsp. fresh thyme leaves
- 1½ tsp. kosher or fine sea salt
- 1 tsp. black pepper
- 1 tsp. ground allspice
- ¼ tsp. ground nutmeg
- 1 (1½-lb.) pork tenderloin
- 2 plantains

PINEAPPLE SALSA

- 1½ cups diced fresh pineapple
- ½ cup fresh cilantro leaves, chopped
- ¼ cup finely diced red onion
- 1 jalapeño pepper, seeded if desired (for less heat), minced
- Juice and finely grated zest of 1 large lime
- Kosher or fine sea salt

PREP

1. Place green onions, white onion, garlic, pepper(s), vinegar, soy sauce, 1 Tbsp. vegetable oil, brown sugar, thyme, salt, pepper, allspice and nutmeg in a blender or food processor and process until smooth.

2. Place the pork loin fat-side down on a cutting board. Using a long, sharp knife, make a horizontal slice lengthwise about ⅓ of the way from the bottom stopping about one inch from the other side. Open the flap. Make another horizontal cut halfway into thicker side of the roast, starting from the center and working toward the outer edge. Open the flap, creating a flat piece of meat. Gently pound with a mallet or rolling pin until even. Place the pork on a baking dish and rub all over with the marinade. Cover with plastic wrap and refrigerate for 4 to 24 hours.

3. Meanwhile, combine all salsa ingredients except salt and mix well. Season to taste with salt. Best made an hour before serving. (Cover and refrigerate for 1 to 24 hours.)

4. Prepare grill for direct and indirect heat, preheat to medium-high and oil the grates. Remove the pork from the marinade and let sit at room temperature while the grill heats. Cut the plantains in half lengthwise and brush with oil. Season with salt and pepper, then place cut side down on the grill over direct heat and grill with the lid closed for 4 to 5 minutes or until charred. Flip over and move to the indirect side.

5. Place the pork on the grill over direct heat and grill with the lid closed for 8 minutes per side or until it reaches an internal temperature of 160 degrees F. Continue to cook the plantains until they are fork tender. Serve with the pineapple salsa.

SERVES 4

BLUE RIBBON SMOKED BOSTON BUTT

We can't promise this recipe will make you a cinch to win the county fair, but don't be surprised if you win the adoring affections of all who pick a piece or 20.

PROVISIONS

Vegetable oil

1 (3–4 lb.) Boston butt

4–6 Tbsp. dry rub (your favorite or see pg. 166)

1–2 cups barbecue sauce (your favorite or see pg. 166)

PREP

1. Preheat a smoker to 275 degrees F (or a grill with indirect heat, see below). Oil the grates.

2. Rub the Boston butt all over with dry rub. Place on the smoker fat side up. Smoke for 5 to 7 hours or until the pork reaches an internal temperature of 195–205 degrees F. Baste with barbecue sauce the last 15 minutes of smoking. Cover liberally with more sauce.

3. May be sliced or shredded for pulled pork sandwiches—simply shred the pork, toss with your favorite barbecue sauce and serve on buns with coleslaw and pickled red onions.

TO COOK ON THE GRILL:

1. Prepare grill for indirect heat and preheat to 275 degrees F. Oil the grates.

2. Rub the Boston butt all over with dry rub. Place on the indirect side of the grill fat side up and close the lid. Grill, maintaining a temperature of 275 degrees F, for 5 to 7 hours or until the pork reaches an internal temperature

of 195–205 degrees F. Baste with barbecue sauce the last 15 minutes of grilling. Cover liberally with more sauce.

SERVES 10

Duke attends the 1949 Los Angeles County Sheriff's Rodeo.

DID YOU KNOW?

As the grand marshal at the 1949 Los Angeles County Sheriff's Rodeo, Duke celebrated the event along with fellow stars Jane Russell and Gene Autry.

Tex Mex Nacho Dogs,
p. 200

BURGERS & DOGS

Handy, flavorsome and easy to grill, these tried-and-true classics cook up in no time and can be customized to suit any palate.

Bacon Burger with Caramelized Onions

Chicken Fajita Burgers

Green Chile Cheeseburgers

Pimento Cheese Burgers

California Burgers

Southwestern Turkey Burgers

Lone Star Chili Cheese Dogs

Tex Mex Nacho Dogs

Rooster's Reuben Dogs

Blazin' Buffalo Dogs

WAYNE FAMILY TIP

Putting an indent in the center of each patty with your thumb prevents the patties from bunching up in the middle. This ensures that your burger cooks evenly, pilgrim!

BACON BURGER
WITH CARAMELIZED ONIONS

With crispy bacon, delicious fixings and a bit of a kick, every bite of this burger bursts with flavor.

PROVISIONS

- ¾ cup mayonnaise
- 2 Tbsp. Sriracha sauce
- 8 slices thick-cut bacon
- 2 lb. ground chuck (80/20)
- Vegetable oil
- Kosher or fine sea salt
- Pepper
- 6 Kaiser rolls
- 3 Tbsp. melted butter
- Store-bought or homemade (recipe below) caramelized onions
- 6 lettuce leaves
- 6 slices tomato

CARAMELIZED ONIONS

- 2½ lb. white or yellow onions (3 large)
- 2 Tbsp. unsalted butter
- 2 Tbsp. olive oil
- ½ tsp. kosher or fine sea salt
- ¼ tsp. pepper
- 4 sprigs fresh thyme
- 2 Tbsp. balsamic vinegar

PREP

1. Combine mayonnaise and Sriracha sauce in a small bowl. Cover and refrigerate until serving time.

2. To prepare the caramelized onions, cut onions in half and slice thinly. In a large skillet over medium-low heat, heat butter and oil together, then add the sliced onions, salt, pepper and thyme, stirring occasionally until the onions are deeply browned and caramelized, about 45 minutes. Remove the thyme sprigs, raise heat to high and add the balsamic vinegar. Cook, stirring, until all the vinegar has evaporated. Store in a covered container in the refrigerator. (Can be made several days ahead.) Reheat in microwave or on stovetop before using.

3. Prepare grill for direct heat and preheat to medium.

4. Dice the bacon into ⅛-inch pieces, then combine with ground chuck, making sure to distribute the bacon evenly through the beef. Divide into six equal portions and shape into patties about ¾-inch thick. Make a depression in the center of each patty with your thumb. Brush both sides of the patties with oil and season with salt and pepper. Grill for 4 minutes, flip the burgers and grill for another 4 to 5 minutes for medium rare.

5. Cut the Kaiser rolls in half, spread the cut surfaces with melted butter and grill for 1 to 2 minutes.

6. To serve, spread the bottom roll with some of the mayonnaise mixture and top with lettuce, tomato slice, burger patty and some caramelized onions.

MAKES 6 BURGERS

John Wayne and Janet Leigh in *Jet Pilot* (1957).

CHICKEN FAJITA BURGERS

Once your guests taste these burgers, they might try to make off with the recipe like a bunch of bandits.

PROVISIONS

- 1 Tbsp. olive oil
- 1 medium white onion, thinly sliced
- 1 green bell pepper, seeded, deveined and thinly sliced
- 1 red bell pepper, seeded, deveined and thinly sliced
- Kosher or fine sea salt
- Pepper
- 2 ripe avocados
- ¼ cup chunky salsa
- Juice of 1 lime
- 1½ lb. ground chicken
- ½ cup grated cheddar cheese
- 4 hamburger buns

PREP

1. In a large skillet over medium-high heat, heat the oil, then add the onion, peppers, ½ tsp. salt and ¼ tsp. pepper. Cook, stirring occasionally, until softened and starting to brown, about 8 minutes. Remove from the pan and set aside.

2. Mash the avocados with the salsa and lime juice; season to taste with salt and pepper.

3. Prepare grill for direct heat and heat to medium-high.

4. Combine the chicken and cheese in a large mixing bowl and divide into four equal sized portions. Form each portion into a patty and make a depression in the center of each patty with your thumb. Brush the patties with oil and season with salt and pepper.

5. Grill the burgers with the lid closed for 4 minutes. Flip and cook another 4 minutes or until the burgers are cooked through.

6. Serve the burgers on buns spread with the avocado mixture and topped with the onion and pepper mixture.

SERVES 4

John Wayne and Ann-Margret in *The Train Robbers* (1973).

GREEN CHILE CHEESEBURGERS

An American classic meets south-of-the-border spice in this show-stealing dish.

PROVISIONS

- 2 (4-oz.) cans diced green chiles, mild or hot
- 2 Tbsp. finely minced onion
- 2 Tbsp. minced cilantro
- 1 tsp. agave nectar
- Kosher or fine sea salt
- Black pepper
- 1½ lb. ground chuck (80/20)
- Vegetable oil
- 4 slices pepper jack cheese
- 4 hamburger buns

John Wayne and LeRoy Mason in *Santa Fe Stampede* (1938).

PREP

1. Combine the chiles with the onion, cilantro, agave, ½ tsp. salt and ¼ tsp. pepper. Set aside.

2. Divide the ground chuck into four equal portions and shape into patties about ¾-inch thick. Make an indentation with your thumb in the middle of the patties. Brush both sides of the patties lightly with oil and season with salt and pepper. Let sit at room temperature while the grill heats.

3. Prepare grill for direct and indirect heat and preheat to medium-high. Oil the grates well. Grill on one side over direct heat with the lid closed for 4 minutes. Flip and grill with the lid closed for another 2 minutes. Move the patties to the indirect side of the grill. Top each patty with a slice of cheese. Close the lid and grill for another 1½ minutes or until the cheese is fully melted.

DID YOU KNOW?

LeRoy Mason (above) appeared with Duke in 10 films, including *California Straight Ahead!* (1937), *Wyoming Outlaw* (1939) and *New Frontier* (1939).

4. If desired, brush the cut sides of the burger buns with oil and toast over the direct side of the grill for 1 to 2 minutes.

5. Place one patty on the bottom of each bun, spoon on the green chile salsa and put on the bun tops.

SERVES 4

PIMENTO CHEESE BURGERS

These ground rounds will give you the fuel you need before you hit the big trail or the big game.

PROVISIONS

- 4 oz. sharp cheddar cheese, grated
- 5 Tbsp. mayonnaise, plus more for the buns
- 2 Tbsp. chopped pimentos
- 3-4 dashes hot sauce
- Vegetable oil
- 1½ lb. ground chuck (80/20)
- Kosher or fine sea salt
- Black pepper
- 4 hamburger buns
- 4 large tomato slices
- 4 iceberg lettuce leaves

PREP

1. Combine the cheese, 5 Tbsp. mayonnaise, pimentos and hot sauce in a food processor and pulse to combine. (Can also be mixed by hand.)

2. Prepare grill for direct heat and preheat to medium-high.

3. Divide the ground chuck into four equal portions, then shape into patties about ¾-inch thick. Make a depression in the center of each patty with your thumb. Brush both sides of the patties with oil and season with salt and pepper.

4. Oil the grill grates.

5. Grill the burger patties for 4 minutes with the lid closed, flip the burgers and grill for another 4 to 5 minutes for medium rare.

6. Brush the burger buns with oil and grill for 1 to 2 minutes to toast.

7. Spread your desired amount of mayonnaise on both cut surfaces of the bun. Assemble each burger by placing a lettuce leaf on the bottom bun, then add tomato, the burger patty and top with the pimento cheese spread.

SERVES 4

Tully Marshall and John Wayne in *The Big Trail* (1930).

CALIFORNIA BURGERS

These tasty burgers live up to the standard of the Golden State.

PROVISIONS

- 3 Tbsp. mayonnaise
- 3 Tbsp. ketchup
- 1½ lb. lean ground chicken or turkey
- 1 Tbsp. ranch seasoning
- Vegetable oil
- Kosher or fine sea salt
- Black pepper
- 2 Tbsp. melted butter
- 4 hamburger buns
- 4 large tomato slices
- 4 iceberg lettuce leaves
- 1 large or 2 small avocados, peeled, seeded and sliced

John Wayne in *California Straight Ahead!* (1937).

PREP

1. Combine the mayonnaise and ketchup in a small bowl.

2. Prepare grill for direct heat and preheat to medium.

3. Mix the ground chicken or turkey with the ranch seasoning mix. Shape into four patties, brush with oil and season with salt and pepper.

4. Oil the grill grates. Grill the burgers with the lid closed until golden brown and cooked through, about 5 minutes per side.

5. Brush the hamburger buns with melted butter and grill 1 to 2 minutes or until lightly toasted.

6. Place your desired amount of the mayonnaise and ketchup mixture on the bottom buns, add lettuce and tomato slices then add the burger. Drizzle with more sauce and top with avocado slices.

SERVES 4

AMERICAN GRILL FACTS

Hamburgers first became popular in the United States after they were served at the 1904 St. Louis World's Fair.

John Wayne in *The Man Who Shot Liberty Valance* (1962).

SOUTHWESTERN TURKEY BURGERS

Let's talk turkey, pilgrim—these spicy burgers are bound to be a hit at your next get-together.

PROVISIONS

- ½ cup mayonnaise
- 1 Tbsp. Sriracha sauce
- 1½ lb. ground turkey
- ½ cup grated cheddar cheese
- Vegetable oil
- Kosher or fine sea salt
- Pepper
- 4 hamburger buns
- 1 avocado, sliced

PREP

1. Combine the mayonnaise and Sriracha sauce in a small bowl. Refrigerate, covered until ready to serve.

2. Prepare grill for direct heat and heat to medium-high.

3. Combine the turkey and cheese in a large mixing bowl and divide into four equal-sized portions. Form each portion into patties and make a depression in the center of each patty with your thumb. Brush the patties with oil; season with salt and pepper.

4. Brush grill grates with oil. Grill the burgers for 4 minutes with the lid closed. Flip and cook another 4 minutes or until the burgers are cooked through.

5. Lightly grill the hamburger buns. Spread a dollop of spicy mayonnaise on each side of the bun. Serve the burgers on the buns with avocado slices.

SERVES 4

DID YOU KNOW?

John Wayne only used the word "pilgrim" in two films: *The Man Who Shot Liberty Valance* (1962) and *McLintock!* (1963).

LONE STAR CHILI CHEESE DOGS

These dogs may be messy, but the best things in life are worth getting your hands dirty for.

PROVISIONS

- 1 **medium white or yellow onion**
- 1 **Tbsp. olive oil**
- 1 **tsp. Kosher or fine sea salt**
- 4 **cloves garlic, minced**
- 1½ **Tbsp. chili powder**
- 1 **tsp. black pepper**
- 1 **tsp. ground cumin**
- ¼ **tsp. allspice**
- ¼ **tsp. cayenne pepper**
- 1 **lb. lean ground beef (85/15)**
- 8 **oz. tomato sauce**
- 4 **oz. water**
- 1 **Tbsp. red wine vinegar**
- 6 **all-beef hot dogs**
- 6 **hot dog buns**
- **Vegetable oil**
- ¾ **cup grated cheddar cheese**

PREP

1. Prepare the grill for direct and indirect heat and preheat to medium-high.

2. Peel and dice the onion. Set aside about a quarter of the onion for serving.

3. Place a cast iron Dutch oven or large skillet over direct heat and let it get hot. Add the olive oil and rest of the onion. Sprinkle the salt over the onion to keep it from browning too much. Cook, stirring occasionally, until softened, about 5 minutes. Add the garlic and cook, stirring for 30 seconds. Add the chili powder, pepper, cumin, allspice and cayenne pepper and cook, stirring until fragrant, about 1 minute. Add the beef and cook, breaking it up with a spoon or spatula. Cook, stirring occasionally, until browned and cooked through, about 8 minutes. Add the tomato sauce, water and vinegar and bring to a simmer. Move the pot to the indirect side of the grill, close the lid and let cook for 20 to 30 minutes, stirring occasionally.

4. Oil the grates of the direct heat side. Oil the hot dogs and buns. Cook the hot dogs for about 7 minutes or until charred and heated through, turning occasionally. Grill the buns, oiled side down, for 1 to 2 minutes. Serve the hot dogs in the buns, topped with chili, cheese and onions.

MAKES 6 HOT DOGS

John Wayne and George "Gabby" Hayes in *Texas Terror* (1935).

TEX MEX NACHO DOGS

These dogs are sure to satisfy your family and friends—even if they've got an appetite the size of the Alamo.

PROVISIONS

- 8 **hot dogs**
- **Vegetable oil**
- 8 **hot dog buns**
- 3 **cups crumbled tortilla chips**
- 2½ **cups shredded Mexican cheese**
- 1 **cup salsa**
- **Pickled jalapeño slices**
- 2 **avocados, sliced**
- ½ **cup sour cream**

PREP

1. Prepare the grill for direct and indirect heat and preheat to medium.

2. Brush the hot dogs as well as the grates on the direct side of the grill with oil. Grill for 3 to 4 minutes or until just charred, turning frequently.

3. Place the grilled hot dogs in the hot dog buns. Sprinkle about 3 Tbsp. of crushed tortilla chips on each hot dog and top with about ¼ cup of cheese.

4. Place a double layer of heavy-duty foil on the indirect side of the grill. Put the hot dogs on the foil, close the lid and cook for 5 to 6 minutes or until the cheese is melted.

5. Top with salsa, jalapeño and avocado slices. Drizzle with sour cream before serving.

MAKES 8 HOT DOGS

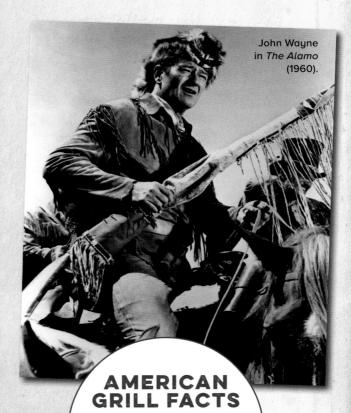

John Wayne in *The Alamo* (1960).

AMERICAN GRILL FACTS

It's estimated that Americans consume 20 billion hot dogs per year, which equates to about 70 dogs per person.

ROOSTER'S REUBEN DOGS

Now you can fill your hand with this iconic deli staple.

PROVISIONS

- ½ cup sour cream
- 6 Tbsp. ketchup
- 1 garlic clove, grated
- 1½ tsp. prepared horseradish
- 2 cups sauerkraut
- 8 all-beef hot dogs
  Vegetable oil
- 8 slices Swiss cheese
- 8 hot dog buns
- 8 dill pickle spears

PREP

1. Combine the sour cream, ketchup, garlic and horseradish. Cover and refrigerate until serving.

2. Prepare grill for direct and indirect heat and preheat to medium-high.

3. Place the sauerkraut in a pan and heat over direct heat until warm. Move to the indirect side to keep warm. (Can also be warmed on the stove.)

4. Brush the grates over direct heat with oil. Place a large piece of heavy-duty foil over the indirect side.

5. Cut the hot dogs lengthwise almost all the way through. Open them up flat and brush both sides with oil. Cut each slice of Swiss cheese into 3 equal lengths. Brush the buns with oil.

6. Grill the hot dogs cut-side down for 2 minutes or until charred, pressing flat with a spatula if needed. Flip over and grill for another 2 minutes. Lay three of the cheese slices on the inside of the hot dogs and then place on the foil over indirect heat. Close the lid and let cook for another 2 minutes or until the cheese is melted. Grill the buns over direct heat for a minute or two to toast.

7. Place the hot dogs in the buns cheese side up. Top with sauerkraut, add a pickle spear and drizzle with the sauce before serving.

MAKES 8 HOT DOGS

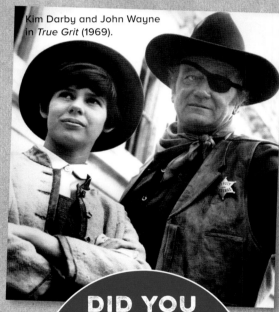

Kim Darby and John Wayne in *True Grit* (1969).

DID YOU KNOW?

When Duke won an Academy Award for his performance in *True Grit* (1969), he quipped, "If I'd have known that, I would have put that eye patch on 35 years earlier."

BLAZIN' BUFFALO DOGS

Hold onto your hat—these dogs have a bite!

PROVISIONS

8   chicken or turkey hot dogs

8   slices bacon (not thick cut)

    Vegetable oil

8   hot dog buns

4   Tbsp. melted butter

¼   cup Buffalo wing sauce
    (recipe below), or your favorite

4   oz. blue cheese, crumbled

1   large celery stalk, very thinly
    sliced on the diagonal

    Ranch dressing

BUFFALO WING SAUCE

1   cup hot sauce

½   cup melted butter

½   tsp. garlic powder

MAKES ABOUT 1½ CUPS

PREP

1. Whisk sauce ingredients to combine.

2. Prepare grill for direct heat and preheat to medium-high.

3. Wrap the bacon around the dogs and secure it at both ends with toothpicks. Brush the hot dog buns with melted butter.

4. Brush the grates with oil. Grill the hot dogs, turning occasionally, until crispy for 6 to 7 minutes. Place the buns on the grill for 1 to 2 minutes to toast.

John Wayne in *Hondo* (1953).

5. Brush the hot dogs with Buffalo sauce and place in the buns. Top with blue cheese, celery and drizzle with ranch dressing.

MAKES 8 HOT DOGS

Cheese-Stuffed Poblano
Peppers with Salsa, p. 240

SIDES

The next best thing to mains, these flavor-packed smaller bites are designed to accompany just about anything you can dish out.

Frontier-Style Vegetable Salad with Bacon

Giddyup Grilled Corn with Chipotle Butter

Eggplant Parmesan Stacks

Duke's Grilled Artichokes

Perfect Grilled Panzanella

Argentinian Grilled Potato Salad

Golden State Grilled Salad

Grilled Asparagus with Toasted Walnuts

Grilled Portobello Mushrooms

Summer Squash Vegetable Foil Packs

Rainbow Valley Vegetable Skewers

Ethan Edwards's Eggplant and Pepper Salad

Grilled Cauliflower Steaks

Un-beet-able Salad

Cheese-Stuffed Poblano Peppers with Salsa

Honey-Orange-Glazed Carrots

Green (Berets) Beans with Lemon Oil

Better Than Good Garlic Bread

FRONTIER-STYLE VEGETABLE SALAD
WITH BACON

Where there's bacon, there's bound to be happy eaters, no ifs, ands or buts about it.

PROVISIONS

- 3 red or yellow peppers (or a combination)
- ¾ cup olive oil
- ⅓ cup balsamic vinegar
- 2 tsp. dried oregano
- 1 tsp. kosher or fine sea salt
- ½ tsp. black pepper
- 1 large or 2 small eggplants
- 1 large white onion, cut into ½-inch slices
- 4 cups arugula
- 4 slices bacon, cooked and crumbled

John Wayne in *The Lawless Frontier* (1934).

PREP

1. Prepare grill for direct heat and preheat to medium-high.

2. Place the peppers on the grill whole and grill with the lid closed until the skin is blackened all over, turning occasionally, about 6 minutes. Remove from the grill, place in a bowl and cover with plastic wrap. Let cool at room temperature.

3. Whisk together the olive oil, vinegar, oregano, salt and pepper.

4. Slice the eggplant into ¼-inch-thick slices. Brush each eggplant slice and onion slice on both sides with the oil and vinegar mixture. Grill with the lid closed until slightly charred and beginning to soften, about 4 to 5 minutes per side. Remove from the grill and brush again with the oil and vinegar mixture. Let cool.

5. When the peppers are cool enough to handle, scrape off the skins and slice in half. Remove the seeds and veins, then cut into ¼-inch thick strips. Brush with the oil and vinegar mixture.

6. Toss the arugula with 3 Tbsp. oil and vinegar mixture. Place the arugula on a platter, top with the grilled vegetables and scatter the bacon over the top before serving.

SERVES 6–8

GIDDYUP GRILLED CORN
WITH CHIPOTLE BUTTER

The smoky, spicy spread for this corn will send your taste buds on a wild ride!

PROVISIONS

- 8 ears corn
- 6 Tbsp. unsalted butter, at room temperature
- 1 Tbsp. pureed chipotles in adobo sauce
- 1 Tbsp. fresh lime juice
- 2 tsp. furikake (or sesame seeds)
- ¼ cup coarsely chopped cilantro

PREP

1. Prepare grill for direct heat and preheat to medium, 350 degrees F.

2. Soak corn in warm water for 10 minutes. Peel back the corn husks, leaving them attached, and remove the silk from the corn. (For a dramatic presentation, separate the husks into thirds and braid.)

3. Combine the butter, chipotles and lime juice. Brush the corn with the butter mixture and grill, turning often and basting with more butter, until the corn is cooked and starting to get grill marks, about 10 minutes.

4. Remove corn to a serving platter, sprinkle with the furikake and cilantro and serve.

SERVES 8

John Wayne with Duke the horse in *Ride Him, Cowboy* (1932).

WAYNE FAMILY TIP

It's rare to use a whole can of chipotles in adobo sauce in one go. To cut down on food waste (and prep time), puree the whole can in a blender, then transfer the mixture to a covered glass container and refrigerate for flavor you can add in a pinch.

EGGPLANT PARMESAN STACKS

When the chips are down and you aren't sure how to win over the dinner crowd, stack the deck in your favor with these pizza-like cheesy bites of grilled eggplant.

PROVISIONS

Vegetable oil

1 large eggplant, cut into eight ½-inch-thick slices

Kosher or fine sea salt

Olive oil

Black pepper

1 lb. fresh mozzarella cheese, sliced into 8 pieces

2 large tomatoes, each cut into 4 thick slices

½ cup shredded Parmesan cheese

Fresh basil leaves

PREP

1. Prepare grill for direct and indirect heat and preheat to medium. Oil the grates with vegetable oil.

2. Sprinkle both sides of the eggplant slices with salt and let sit for 5 minutes. Blot dry with paper towels. Brush with olive oil on both sides and sprinkle lightly with pepper.

3. Place the eggplant slices over direct heat and grill with the lid closed for 4 to 6 minutes or until tender. Remove from grill. Top the grilled eggplant slices with mozzarella cheese, tomato slices and Parmesan cheese. Place on the grill over indirect heat and grill with the lid closed for 2 to 3 minutes or until the cheese melts.

4. Top with basil leaves and serve.

MAKES 8 STACKS

Duke takes in the sights while visiting Rome in 1965.

AMERICAN GRILL FACTS

According to the Federal Census of Agriculture, New Jersey grows more eggplants than any other state in the U.S. (California is second).

DUKE'S GRILLED ARTICHOKES

Elegant but delightfully simple, this delectable side is the stuff legends are made of and makes any get-together a meal to remember.

PROVISIONS

- 2 medium lemons, quartered
- 6 large artichokes
- 1 head of garlic
  Kosher or fine sea salt
  Freshly ground black pepper
- ¾ cup mayonnaise

PREP

1. Place lemons in a large bowl of cold water. Cut the very top and bottom off of each artichoke. Using scissors, snip the sharp points off the leaves. Rinse the artichokes, then cut each artichoke into quarters vertically. With a sharp paring knife or spoon, cut the thistle out of each quarter. Drop the artichokes into the lemon water to prevent browning.

2. Prepare grill for indirect heat and preheat to medium.

3. Lay out a large piece of heavy-duty aluminum foil. Remove the artichokes from the water, then shake them dry. Place them in the center of the foil along with the lemon wedges. Cut the top off the head of garlic before tossing the garlic in the foil. Sprinkle with salt and pepper and wrap the foil tightly around the whole lot. Take another large piece of foil and wrap it tightly around the packet so that steam will build up while cooking.

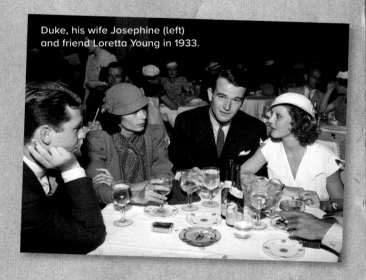

Duke, his wife Josephine (left) and friend Loretta Young in 1933.

4. Place on the grill, close the lid and cook over indirect heat for 50 to 60 minutes or until the leaves of the artichokes pull off easily.

5. Carefully open the foil and place the artichokes and lemon wedges on a serving platter.

6. Squeeze the garlic cloves into the mayonnaise and mix. Serve as a dipping sauce for the artichokes.

SERVES 6

PERFECT GRILLED PANZANELLA

What's panzanella, you ask? This refreshing Italian bread salad gets a new life on the grill and is bursting with juicy slices of tomatoes, onion and cucumber. Serve it on a hot summer day to cool off the Tuscan way.

PROVISIONS

- 1 **baguette**
- **Kosher or fine sea salt**
- ½ **cup olive oil, plus more for brushing the bread and peppers**
- 2 **yellow bell peppers**
- 1 **pint cherry tomatoes, halved**
- 1 **seedless cucumber, chopped**
- ½ **small red onion, thinly sliced**
- 20 **basil leaves**
- 3 **Tbsp. white wine vinegar**
- 1 **garlic clove, minced**
- ½ **tsp. pepper**

PREP

1. Prepare grill for direct heat and preheat to medium-high.

2. Slice the baguette in half, brush with olive oil and sprinkle with salt. Slice the peppers in half, pull out the seeds and veins, then brush with olive oil.

3. Grill the bread for 2 to 3 minutes or until it is charred. Grill the peppers, cut side down, until they are charred and begin to soften, about 4 minutes.

4. Cut the bread into bite-sized pieces and place in a salad bowl. Chop the peppers and add to the bread. Add the tomatoes, cucumber and onion. Stack the basil leaves on

John Wayne and Sophia Loren on the set of *Legend of the Lost* (1957).

a cutting board, roll up like a cigar and thinly slice. Add to the bread and vegetables.

5. In a small bowl, whisk ½ cup olive oil, vinegar, garlic, 1 tsp. salt and pepper. Pour over the salad and toss. Serve or allow to sit at room temperature for 30 minutes to let the flavors meld.

SERVES 6–8

ARGENTINIAN GRILLED POTATO SALAD

Sometimes you need to shake things up. For a taste of the Andes you can savor from the comfort of your patio, this filling, chimichurri-style dish will have your guests raving for more.

PROVISIONS

- 12 medium red potatoes (about 2½ lb.), washed, unpeeled and cut into 1-inch pieces
- 1 medium red onion (about ½ lb.), peeled and diced
- 6 garlic cloves, peeled and cut into quarters
- 6 Tbsp. butter or dairy-free butter substitute, cut into small pieces
- 2 lemons, each cut into thirds
- 1 Tbsp. plus 1 tsp. smoked paprika, divided

  Kosher salt

  Freshly ground black pepper

- ¼ cup mayonnaise or vegan mayonnaise substitute
- ¼ cup extra-virgin olive oil
- ¼ cup sherry vinegar
- ¼ cup flat leaf parsley, chopped

John Wayne and Ella Raines in *Tall in the Saddle* (1944).

PREP

1. Prepare grill for indirect heat and preheat to medium-high.

2. Cut six pieces of foil into 12- by 12-inch squares. On each piece of foil, layer two cut-up potatoes, ⅙ of the onion, one quartered garlic clove and 1 Tbsp. of butter, in that order. Squeeze the juice of ⅓ of a lemon over each. Season each with a dash of smoked paprika and a large pinch of salt and pepper. Fold the foil into tight packets and place over indirect heat. Close the lid and grill for 35 to 45 minutes or until the potatoes are tender.

3. While the potatoes are cooking, whisk together the mayonnaise, olive oil, vinegar, 1 Tbsp. smoked paprika and a large pinch of salt and pepper.

4. To serve, open the foil packets, then spoon some sauce on top of the potatoes. Garnish with parsley.

SERVES 6

John Wayne and Henry Fonda in *In Harm's Way* (1965). Fonda was also Duke's co-star in *Fort Apache* (1948), *The Longest Day* (1962) and *How the West Was Won* (1962).

GOLDEN STATE GRILLED SALAD

If you're hankering for something light and satisfying, this tasty, California-inspired side doesn't skimp on flavor.

PROVISIONS

- ½ cup balsamic vinegar
- 3 heads romaine lettuce hearts, washed and dried well
- 1 medium white onion (about ½ lb.)
-    Extra-virgin olive oil
-    Kosher salt and coarsely ground black pepper
- 4 oz. goat cheese, crumbled

PREP

1. Pour the vinegar into a small saucepan and bring to a boil. Let boil until it's reduced by half and is thick and syrupy, about 10 minutes. Remove from heat and let cool.

2. Leaving the root ends attached, cut the romaine lettuce hearts into quarters vertically. Cut the onion in half vertically and remove the peels. Cut each onion half into six vertical slices. Brush the lettuce quarters with olive oil and toss the onion slices with olive oil.

3. Prepare grill for direct heat and preheat to medium-high. Grill the lettuce quarters for about 1 to 2 minutes on each side. You want them to start to brown but not to get too soft. Remove and transfer to a platter. Grill the onion slices until browned and soft, about 5 minutes. Scatter over the lettuce quarters. Drizzle the balsamic syrup over the lettuce and onions. Drizzle with olive oil, season with salt and pepper and top with the crumbled goat cheese.

SERVES 6

John Wayne and Louise Latimer in *California Straight Ahead!* (1937).

DID YOU KNOW?

Although Duke was born in Iowa, the Morrison family relocated to California in 1914, a state Duke called home for the rest of his life.

GRILLED ASPARAGUS
WITH TOASTED WALNUTS

This succulent garden vegetable has been enjoyed by fans of food for millennia, and with this recipe, it tastes better than ever (and cooks in 5 minutes flat).

PROVISIONS

- 1   lb. large asparagus
- 2   Tbsp. olive oil
- 1   tsp. kosher or fine sea salt
- ½   tsp. black pepper
-     Vegetable oil
- 1   Tbsp. melted butter
- ¼   cup toasted walnut pieces

PREP

1. Prepare grill for direct heat and preheat to medium-high.

2. Cut off the tough woody ends of the asparagus. Toss with olive oil, salt and pepper. Place in an oiled grill pan. Grill the asparagus over direct heat with the lid closed for 5 minutes on each side.

3. Toss the asparagus with melted butter and top with walnut pieces. Serve.

SERVES 4

John Wayne and Elizabeth Allen in *Donovan's Reef* (1963).

GRILLED PORTOBELLO MUSHROOMS

Soaked in a balsamic vinegar and soy sauce marinade, these mouthwatering mushrooms make for the meatiest-tasting meatless option around. If that's your thing.

PROVISIONS

4	large portobello mushrooms
¼	cup balsamic vinegar
2	Tbsp. olive oil
1	Tbsp. soy sauce
1	clove garlic, minced
1	tsp. minced fresh rosemary leaves
½	tsp. black pepper
	Vegetable oil
2	cups baby arugula
2	oz. soft goat cheese, crumbled

PREP

1. Remove the stems and gills from the mushrooms and wipe each mushroom clean with a damp cloth.

2. In a 9- by 12-inch baking dish, combine the vinegar, olive oil, soy sauce, garlic, rosemary and pepper. Whisk until well mixed. Add the mushrooms to the dish. Let sit for 5 minutes, flip them over and let sit while the grill heats.

3. Prepare grill for direct heat and preheat to medium. Oil the grates. Reserving the marinade, place the mushrooms on the grill gill side down. Close the lid and grill for 6 minutes. Flip and grill for 4 to 5 minutes or until tender.

4. Toss the arugula with the reserved marinade and place on a platter. Slice the mushrooms and place on top of the arugula. Top with crumbled goat cheese before serving.

SERVES 4

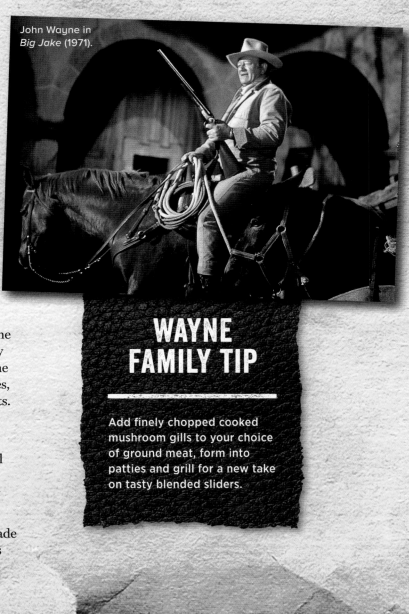

John Wayne in *Big Jake* (1971).

WAYNE FAMILY TIP

Add finely chopped cooked mushroom gills to your choice of ground meat, form into patties and grill for a new take on tasty blended sliders.

SUMMER SQUASH VEGETABLE FOIL PACKS

What's summertime without a little relaxation? Pop these Italian-style vegetables in foil and prop your feet up while you let the grill do the work. We'll tip our hat to that.

PROVISIONS

- 6 Tbsp. olive oil
- 2 Tbsp. red wine vinegar
- 1 tsp. Italian seasoning
- 1 tsp. kosher or fine sea salt
- ¼ tsp. crushed red pepper flakes
- 1 yellow squash, cut into 1-inch pieces
- 1 zucchini, cut into 1-inch pieces
- 1 red, yellow or orange bell pepper, cut into 1-inch pieces
- 1 cup cherry or grape tomatoes
- 1 cup diced red onion
- 4 12- by 18-inch pieces heavy duty aluminum foil
- Nonstick cooking spray
- 2 oz. (½ cup) crumbled feta cheese
- ¼ cup fresh basil leaves, chopped

Duke plays with his dogs at home, 1952.

PREP

1. Prepare the grill for direct heat and preheat to medium.

2. In a large bowl, whisk together the oil, vinegar, Italian seasoning, salt and red pepper flakes. Add the vegetables and toss.

3. Spray the foil pieces with cooking spray. Divide the vegetables evenly among the foil packets. Drizzle the dressing on top of the vegetables. Fold the long sides of foil toward each other and crimp the edges to seal. Fold and crimp the remaining edges to form a sealed packet.

4. Place the foil packets on the grill, close the lid and grill for 12 to 15 minutes. To check for doneness, remove one packet from the grill and unseal carefully. The vegetables should be crisp tender.

5. To serve, cut an X in each packet, then top with the crumbled feta and basil.

MAKES 4 PACKETS

RAINBOW VALLEY VEGETABLE SKEWERS

Make the most of your summer harvest by threading these skewers with eye-catching peppers and savory squash.

PROVISIONS

- 16 wooden skewers
- ¼ cup low sodium soy sauce
- 2 Tbsp. honey
- 1 Tbsp. sesame oil
- 4 cloves garlic, grated
- 1 Tbsp. grated fresh ginger
- ½ tsp. black pepper
- 1 yellow squash, cut into 1-inch pieces
- 1 zucchini, cut into 1-inch pieces
- 8 oz. button mushrooms, wiped clean and ends trimmed
- 2 red, yellow or orange peppers, cut into chunks
- 1 red onion, cut into chunks
- 1 pint cherry tomatoes
- Vegetable oil

John Wayne in *Rainbow Valley* (1935).

PREP

1. Soak the skewers in water for 30 minutes.

2. Meanwhile, combine the soy sauce, honey, sesame oil, garlic, ginger and pepper in a small bowl.

3. Thread the vegetables onto the skewers. Place on a half sheet pan or baking dish. Brush generously with the sauce.

4. Prepare grill for direct heat and preheat to medium. Oil the grates.

5. Place the skewers on the grill and cook, turning and brushing with the sauce every 2 to 3 minutes, until the vegetables are tender, 8 to 10 minutes.

SERVES 8

John Wayne with his wife Pilar and children Aissa and Patrick on the set of *McLintock!* (1963). Patrick appeared in 10 of his father's films, and Aissa appeared in four.

ETHAN EDWARDS'S EGGPLANT AND PEPPER SALAD

Loaded with bold peppery flavor and hearty slices of grilled eggplant, consider your search for the perfect side dish over, pilgrim.

PROVISIONS

- 1 medium eggplant
- 1 medium zucchini
- 1 medium yellow squash
- 8 Tbsp. olive oil, divided
- 1 tsp. kosher or fine sea salt
- ½ tsp. black pepper
- 1 red bell pepper
- Vegetable oil
- 2 Tbsp. balsamic glaze, store bought or homemade, see Step 1
- ¼ cup toasted pine nuts
- 8 Kalamata olives, pitted and sliced
- ¼ fresh basil leaves

PREP

1. If opting to make your own glaze, place ½ cup balsamic vinegar in a small saucepan and bring to a boil over high heat. Reduce heat to a simmer and cook uncovered, stirring occasionally, until the mixture is syrupy and reduced to about 2 Tbsp., about 12 to 15 minutes.

2. Prepare grill for direct heat and preheat to medium-high.

3. Slice the eggplant, zucchini and squash into ¼-inch slices. Place in a bowl with 7 Tbsp. olive oil, salt and pepper. Toss to coat and let sit.

4. Place the bell pepper directly on the grill, turning every 2 to 3 minutes until completely charred all over, about 10 to 12 minutes. Place the pepper in a bowl and cover with a plate. Let sit until cool enough to handle.

5. Oil the grates. Place the eggplant, zucchini and squash slices on the grill and cook until marked and softened, about 4 minutes on each side. Remove and place on a platter.

6. When the pepper is cool enough to handle, remove the skin. Cut in half and remove the seeds and veins. Slice into ¼- to ½-inch strips. Place on top of the other vegetables. Drizzle with the remaining Tbsp. of olive oil and the balsamic glaze. Top with pine nuts, olives and basil leaves.

SERVES 8

John Wayne in
The Searchers (1956).

WAYNE FAMILY TIP

Get the most out of your homemade balsamic glaze by drizzling it over steak, berries, bruschetta and pizza, or up the haute cuisine factor by serving it as part of a cheese plate.

GRILLED CAULIFLOWER STEAKS

Even though Duke had quite a taste for red meat, we're sure he'd get a kick out of this stand-in for steak that comes smothered in queso and salsa for extra south-of-the-border flavor.

PROVISIONS

- 1 tsp. garlic powder
- 1 tsp. chili powder
- 1 tsp. paprika
- 1 tsp. kosher or fine sea salt
- ½ tsp. pepper
- Vegetable oil
- 2 large heads of cauliflower
- 4 Tbsp. olive oil
- ½ cup salsa
- Cilantro leaves, for garnish
- 8 oz. queso (see right)

PREP

1. Combine the garlic powder, chili powder, paprika, salt and pepper in a small bowl.

2. Prepare grill for direct heat and preheat to medium. Oil the grates.

3. Remove the outer leaves from the heads of the cauliflower and trim the stems so the heads sit flat (be careful not to cut too much of the stem). Place each head cut side down on a cutting board, then slice about ⅓ off each side and discard. Slice the rest of the cauliflower into three equal slices, about 1 inch thick.

4. Lay the steaks flat. Brush with olive oil and sprinkle the spice mixture evenly on both sides.

5. Grill for 5 minutes on each side with the lid closed.

6. Heat the queso, then drizzle some over the cauliflower steaks. Serve the rest on the side. Top the cauliflower steaks with salsa and garnish with cilantro leaves before serving.

MAKES 6 CAULIFLOWER STEAKS

HOMEMADE QUESO

Combine 1 (10-oz.) can diced tomatoes and green chiles, undrained and 16 oz. processed American cheese (such as Velveeta) cut into ½-inch cubes in a medium saucepan over medium heat, stirring, until the cheese is fully melted. Makes 16 oz. of queso.

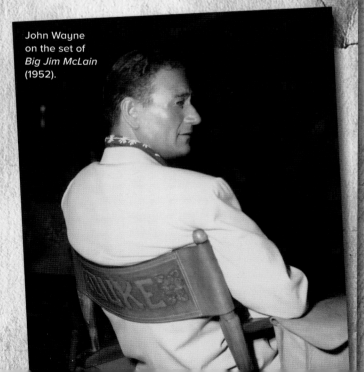

John Wayne on the set of *Big Jim McLain* (1952).

UN-BEET-ABLE SALAD

When you want to serve up a heaping bowl of something healthy, this flavorsome, dark red salad that's as tasty as it is nutritious has you covered.

PROVISIONS

- 8 small red beets
- Olive oil
- Kosher or fine sea salt
- Black pepper
- 1 Tbsp. red wine vinegar
- 2 oz. soft goat cheese
- 2 Tbsp. toasted pumpkin seeds

PREP

1. Prepare the grill for direct and indirect heat. Oil the grates of the direct side. Wrap beets in foil and place on the indirect side of the grill. Close the lid and cook for 20 minutes or until tender. Let cool.

2. When cool enough to handle, rub off the skins of the beets and slice about ¼ inch thick. Brush both sides of the beets with olive oil and place over direct heat for 2 to 3 minutes or until grill marks begin to show.

3. Combine 3 Tbsp. olive oil with the vinegar and a large pinch of salt and pepper. Toss the beets with the dressing and arrange on a plate or platter. Crumble the goat cheese over the top and sprinkle with the pumpkin seeds before serving.

SERVES 4

John Wayne and Rock Hudson in *The Undefeated* (1969).

WAYNE FAMILY TIP

To avoid stains while handling beets, line your cutting board with parchment paper and wear latex gloves while slicing.

CHEESE-STUFFED POBLANO PEPPERS WITH SALSA

For a lighter take on chiles rellenos, skip the meat and forgo the frying pan by popping these cheesy peppers straight onto the grill.

PROVISIONS

- ½ cup roughly chopped white onion
- 2 cloves garlic, roughly chopped
- ½ cup fresh cilantro leaves
- ½ tsp. kosher or fine sea salt
- ½ tsp. garlic powder
- 1 (14.5-oz.) can fire-roasted diced tomatoes, drained
- 1 (10-oz.) can diced tomatoes and green chiles, drained
- 2 Tbsp. fresh lime juice (from 1 large lime)
  Vegetable oil
- 8 large poblano peppers
- 24 oz. shredded Mexican blend cheese

PREP

1. Place onion, garlic, cilantro, salt and garlic powder in a food processor or blender and process until finely chopped.

2. Add the fire-roasted tomatoes, tomatoes and chiles and lime juice and pulse several times until blended but chunky. Allow to sit at room temperature for 30 minutes to let the flavors mingle. (Note: Any leftover salsa can be stored, covered, in the refrigerator for up to two weeks.)

3. Prepare grill for direct and indirect heat and preheat to medium. Oil the grates.

4. Place the peppers over direct heat and grill for 10 to 15 minutes, flipping often, until charred. Place in a bowl and cover with a plate or plastic wrap and let steam until cool enough to handle. Peel the peppers, slit each one from stem to tip and scrape out the seeds.

5. Stuff each pepper with the cheese. Place a large sheet of heavy duty foil over indirect heat, place the peppers on top and grill until the cheese is fully melted, 6 to 8 minutes. Serve with the salsa.

MAKES 8 PEPPERS

HONEY-ORANGE-GLAZED CARROTS

From picky ranch hands to proud carnivores, no one can resist grabbing two or three helpings of these lip-smacking caramelized carrots.

PROVISIONS

Vegetable oil

2 lb. whole carrots with tops

Olive oil

Kosher or fine sea salt

Black pepper

1 large orange

½ cup honey

3 Tbsp. unsalted butter

PREP

1. Prepare grill for direct and indirect heat and preheat to medium-high. Oil the grates with vegetable oil.

2. Cut off all but 1 inch of the carrot tops. Finely chop about ½ cup of the carrot tops and reserve for later. Peel the carrots—if any are larger than 1 inch in diameter, cut those in half lengthwise. Toss with olive oil and season lightly with salt and pepper.

3. Finely grate 1 tsp. of orange zest and squeeze 3 Tbsp. of juice. Place in a saucepan along with the honey, butter, 1 tsp. salt and ½ tsp. pepper.

4. Place the saucepan and carrots over direct heat. Let cook, stirring, until everything is combined. Move to the indirect side of the grill to keep warm.

5. Cook the carrots over direct heat, rotating every 2 minutes, until the carrots are charred on all sides and fork tender, about 15 to 20 minutes. If they begin to get too charred before they're tender, move the carrots to the indirect side of the grill.

6. Brush with the glaze and continue to cook over direct heat for 1 minute. Remove the carrots from the grill and brush again with the glaze. Top with the reserved carrot tops and serve.

SERVES 8

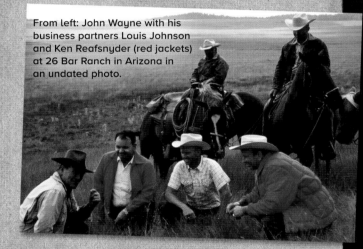

From left: John Wayne with his business partners Louis Johnson and Ken Reafsnyder (red jackets) at 26 Bar Ranch in Arizona in an undated photo.

DID YOU KNOW?

John Wayne hired a legend of a different sort at 26 Bar Ranch: livestock behavior expert Dr. Temple Grandin, who pioneered the curved cattle chute.

GREEN (BERETS) BEANS
WITH LEMON OIL

When you need a reliable side that will complement just about any plate, this citrusy dish is the real deal.

PROVISIONS

Vegetable oil

4 Tbsp. olive oil, divided

1 Tbsp. freshly squeezed lemon juice

2 tsp. minced shallot

1 tsp. Dijon mustard

Kosher or fine sea salt

Black pepper

1½ lb. green beans, trimmed

PREP

1. Prepare grill for direct heat and preheat to medium-high. Oil the grates with vegetable oil.

2. Combine 3 Tbsp. olive oil with the lemon juice, shallot, mustard, ½ tsp. salt and ¼ tsp. pepper in a small jar. Shake well to combine.

3. Wash and dry the green beans. Place in a large mixing bowl, add 1 Tbsp. olive oil and mix to coat the beans with the oil.

4. Place the beans directly on the grates and grill for 4 to 5 minutes, then flip and grill for another 4 to 5 minutes or until the beans are charred and tender. Toss with the dressing and serve.

SERVES 6

John Wayne in *The Green Berets* (1968).

AMERICAN GRILL FACTS

The top three states in America that produce the most green beans (aka snap beans) are Wisconsin, Florida and New York.

BETTER THAN GOOD GARLIC BREAD

This buttery, crunchy bread is so darn delicious, you'll be tempted to serve it with every meal.

PROVISIONS

- 8 Tbsp. unsalted butter, at room temperature
- 2 Tbsp. minced fresh parsley
- 1 Tbsp. minced garlic (3 cloves)
- ½ tsp. kosher or fine sea salt
- 2 baguettes

PREP

1. Prepare grill for direct heat and preheat to medium.

2. Combine the butter, parsley, garlic and salt in a small bowl, mixing well.

3. Cut the baguettes in half horizontally and spread the cut sides with the garlic butter. Put the halves back together, wrap each baguette tightly in heavy duty aluminum foil and place on the grill. Grill, turning occasionally, for 10 to 12 minutes or until the bread is warmed through and the outside is crispy. Slice and serve.

SERVES 6–8

Duke and Dean Martin have fun in the kitchen during the shooting of *The Sons of Katie Elder* (1965).

DID YOU KNOW?

Before co-starring in *The Sons of Katie Elder* (1965), Dean Martin appeared with Duke as Dude in the 1959 Howard Hawks Western *Rio Bravo*.

CONVERSION GUIDE

THEY MEASURE THINGS A LITTLE DIFFERENTLY OVERSEAS, SO USE THIS HANDY CHART TO EXPORT ALL THE CLASSICS THIS AMERICAN GRILL BOOK HAS TO OFFER.

VOLUME	
¼ tsp.	1 mL
½ tsp.	2 mL
1 tsp.	5 mL
1 Tbsp.	15 mL
¼ cup	50mL
⅓ cup	75 mL
½ cup	125 mL
⅔ cup	150 mL
¾ cup	175 mL
1 cup	250 mL
1 quart	1 liter
1½ quarts	1.5 liters
2 quarts	2 liters
2½ quarts	2.5 liters
3 quarts	3 liters
4 quarts	4 liters

TEMPERATURE	
32° F	0° C
212° F	100° C
250° F	120° C
275° F	140° C
300° F	150° C
325° F	160° C
350° F	180° C
375° F	190° C
400° F	200° C
425° F	220° C
450° F	230° C
475° F	250° C
500° F	260° C

WEIGHT	
1 oz.	30 g
2 oz.	55 g
3 oz.	85 g
4 oz / ¼ lb.	115 g
8 oz / ½ lb.	225 g
16 oz / 1 lb.	455 g
2 lb.	905 g

LENGTH	
⅛ in.	3 mm
¼ in.	6 mm
½ in.	13 mm
¾ in.	19 mm
1 in.	2.5 cm
2 in.	5 cm

John Wayne in
Red River (1948).

INDEX

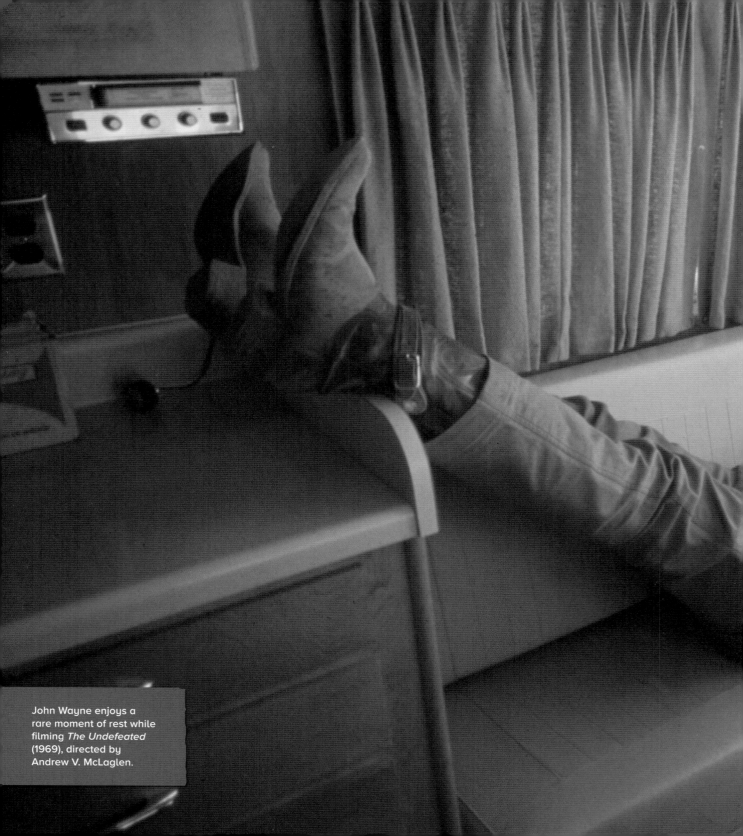

John Wayne enjoys a
rare moment of rest while
filming *The Undefeated*
(1969), directed by
Andrew V. McLaglen.

Media Lab Books
For inquiries, call 646-838-6637

Copyright 2022 Topix Media Lab

Published by Topix Media Lab
14 Wall Street, Suite 4B
New York, NY 10005

Printed in Korea

ISBN-13: 978-1-948174-89-3
ISBN-10: 1-948174-89-8

Vice President & Publisher Phil Sexton
Senior Vice President of Sales & New Markets Tom Mifsud
Vice President of Retail Sales & Logistics Linda Greenblatt
Chief Financial Officer Vandana Patel
Manufacturing Director Nancy Puskuldjian
Financial Analyst Matthew Quinn
Digital Marketing & Strategy Manager Elyse Gregov

Chief Content Officer Jeff Ashworth
Director of Editorial Operations Courtney Kerrigan
Creative Director Susan Dazzo
Photo Director Dave Weiss
Executive Editor Tim Baker

Content Editor Juliana Sharaf
Senior Editor Trevor Courneen
Assistant Managing Editor Tara Sherman
Designers Glen Karpowich, Mikio Sakai
Copy Editor & Fact Checker Madeline Raynor
Junior Designer Alyssa Bredin Quirós

Recipes and recipe photography by Carol Kicinsky and Kate Walker

Indexing by R studio T, NYC